# Growing in Grace

# Growing in Grace

*Becoming More Like Jesus*

Banner Mini-Guides
*Christian Living*

Jonathan Master

THE BANNER OF TRUTH TRUST

# THE BANNER OF TRUTH TRUST

*Head Office*
3 Murrayfield Road
Edinburgh, EH12 6EL
UK

*North America Office*
PO Box 621
Carlisle, PA 17013
USA

banneroftruth.org

© The Banner of Truth Trust, 2020

ISBN
Print: 978 1 84871 931 6
EPUB: 978 1 84871 932 3
Kindle: 978 1 84871 933 0

\*

Typeset in 10/14 pt Minion Pro
at the Banner of Truth Trust, Edinburgh

Printed in the USA by
Versa Press, Inc.,
East Peoria, IL

For
Caroline and Taylor

# Contents

# Introduction

This book is written with two basic assumptions in mind. The first is that Christians – repentant sinners really trusting in Christ alone for their forgiveness and standing with God – ought to be growing in their faith. If you are a Christian and you are not growing, then something is very seriously wrong. There is an analogy here with biological life. If a baby or an infant fails to grow, the doctors become gravely concerned. If a plant will not grow, then any competent gardener will know that something needs to change. So it is with our Christian lives. Christians are meant to grow.

The second assumption is closely related to the first. Not only are Christians meant to grow, our growth is a product of the grace of God. No Christian will ever see the Lord in heaven and be able to boast about having accomplished something independent of him. Our lives, from beginning to end, are monuments to the grace of God. Christians should be growing, and that growth is explained in the Bible as growth in grace.

In order to understand this important subject more clearly, this book has been divided into four parts. In

Part 1 we will look at the broad contours of growth in grace. This outline of grace will first deal with the phrase 'growth in grace' itself, then with the nature of our salvation and finally it will give a brief sketch or portrait of a figure in the Bible who is an illustration of what growth in grace entails.

In Part 2 we will give our attention to the Lord Jesus Christ. As we will see, the Bible sometimes refers to Jesus' incarnation simply as the 'coming of grace'. By examining Jesus' role as our prophet, priest, and king we will see not only the way in which he showcases God's grace in his coming but also how he continues to govern and guide us as we grow in grace today.

Part 3 will focus on some of the means of grace that God has given. When Jesus Christ was physically present on the earth he ordained several means by which Christians are to grow in grace. Specifically, we will examine briefly the Lord's Supper and the church. We will touch briefly on baptism as well, though some of the biblical teachings on this subject cannot be dealt with in a book of this size.

Finally, in Part 4 we will look at the very specific ways in which the Bible talks about our Christian growth. What we will see is that God has not only provided us with the provision to grow as Christians, he has also provided careful instruction about how we ought to view ourselves and our circumstances as we live a life of grace.

Undertaking a book such as this is a humbling experience. My own Christian life does not provide an example of steady and unbroken application of the teachings I have sought to explain. As we will see, however, growth in grace is never an individual experience; Christians are meant to grow together. And all of us can attest to the powerful work of our Saviour and friend, Jesus Christ, in the midst of our pilgrim journey.

JONATHAN MASTER
Morrisville, PA, 2019

# PART 1

## AN OUTLINE OF GRACE

# 1

# Grow in Grace
# 2 Peter 3:18

## Last words

Last words are significant. They often provide a window into the priorities of an individual's life. If we know someone is about to die we often gather at the bedside, not only to give comfort, but perhaps also to receive some kind of wisdom. Not everyone is lucid at the end of life, of course, but it is remarkable to note how often these last words do convey a profound truth.

There are many famous accounts of an individual's last words. These range from the banal and sad to the hopeful and profound. Humphrey Bogart is said to have remarked, 'I should never have switched from Scotch to Martinis.' With similar frivolity, Oscar Wilde declared, 'Either this wallpaper goes or I go.' The great British statesman Winston Churchill is reported to have said, 'I'm so bored with it all.' What a deeply melancholy note to strike at the end of such an eventful life! At the other end of the spectrum, the American New Testament scholar J. Gresham Machen's last words were written as part of a telegram to his dear colleague John Murray. Machen wrote: 'I'm so thankful for the active obedience of Christ. No hope without it.'

Even in the Bible, last words are significant. The last words of the patriarchs of Israel often had deep and abiding prophetic significance. And on an entirely different scale, we recognize in the last words of Jesus Christ on the cross many of the significant themes regarding his life, death, and resurrection.

The same is true with the last recorded words of one of Jesus' apostles. Peter was with Jesus from the beginning of his earthly ministry. He was one of three men chosen to accompany Jesus up to the Mount of Transfiguration. He was with Jesus in the upper room during the Last Supper. He was near Jesus when he died, though he shamefully claimed no association with the Lord during that hour of testing.

Peter was also the primary preacher on the Day of Pentecost, forty days after Jesus' ascent into heaven. He was the one who explained the work of the Holy Spirit to those gathered in Jerusalem on that eventful day. He rubbed shoulders with the apostle Paul, and was even rebuked by him during the early days of the church in Antioch. He was a leader in the early church, having been present from the days of Jesus' earthly ministry.

Of course, all Scripture is inspired and profitable, but with all of Peter's experience and background, we would expect his last recorded words to be especially poignant, summarizing a lifetime of service to Christ. The words come to us in 2 Peter 3:18: 'But grow in the grace and knowledge of our Lord and Saviour Jesus Christ. To him be the glory both now and to the day of eternity. Amen.'

It is worth thinking carefully about Peter's last words. His last words ascribe all glory to Jesus Christ. As we will see, this needs to be our pre-eminent focus as well in the Christian life. Our very existence as creatures of God is meant to bring glory to Jesus Christ. Peter recognizes that. Even after Peter's many 'accomplishments' in ministry, after all his important leadership roles, notwithstanding his time with the Lord on earth, it is Christ alone who ought to receive the glory.

But before this statement of praise Peter gives a command and that final command revolves around two concepts: grace and knowledge. These two seem to go together in Peter's mind. They are what we might call 'a package deal.' And they are things that Christians are commanded to grow in.

### Grace and knowledge

First, *grace*. Grace has been defined as 'unmerited favour'. It is something given to us that is undeserved. In the Bible, this is an incredibly important concept. From the very beginning of Genesis, God is shown to be a God of grace. He did not have to give Adam and Eve everything that he gave them in the garden. Certainly he did not have to clothe them and give them promises after they had sinned. But he did. And again and again, God is shown to be a God of grace.

Our salvation is said to be of grace. It is a gift that is unearned. Paul reminds us of this in Ephesians 2:8, 9, contrasting the notion of our works with that of God's grace: 'For by grace you have been saved through faith. And this is not your own doing; it is the gift of God, not a result of works, so that no one may boast.' In fact, our relationship with God, from beginning to end, is a testimony of his grace.

But if grace is unmerited favour, how could we possibly be commanded to grow in it? After all, it is not something from *us* at all! There are two answers to this question. The first is that growth in grace is another way of saying growth in Christlikeness. Many people have observed that the apostle Paul frequently uses the term 'grace' simply as a way of describing the revelation of God in the person of Jesus Christ. He writes in Titus 2:11: 'For the grace of God has appeared, bringing salvation for all people... '. As we continue to read Paul's letter to Titus, we see that when he refers here to the appearing of 'grace,' he really means the appearing of Jesus (see Titus 3:4). In other words, grace is not some kind of substance imparted to us impersonally, but it is a reality personified and mediated by the living Lord Jesus Christ. To grow in grace is to grow into conformity to the one who is himself the living embodiment of grace. Here it is worth remembering the 'package deal' which Peter introduces: grace and *knowledge of the Lord Jesus Christ*. This is why so much of our thinking on this subject needs to be focused on Jesus Christ and his work. He, as our saviour, example and mediator, needs to be at the very centre of everything we think concerning this great topic.

But there is also another related truth upon which this command touches. We can be commanded to grow in grace because the Bible gives us clear direction about the way in which God graciously causes this in us. Because the Scriptures are clear about the way in which Christian maturity is pursued and fostered, and because the Scriptures are equally clear about the fact that our growth comes as a result of God's work, then the command to 'grow in grace' has substance and intelligibility.

Perhaps an example from the life of the apostle Paul will help. In 1 Corinthians 15, Paul explained how his apostleship compared with that of the other apostles of Jesus Christ. Among other things, Paul was the 'least' and 'last' of the apostles. But as Paul described his work in the gospel ministry, he wrote this: 'I worked harder than any of them, though it was not I, but the grace of God that is with me.' Do you see this dynamic? Paul worked hard. He made every effort, and he needed to use all the energy he possessed to do it. Yet at the same time, he attributes his work to the grace of God.

Growing in grace requires hard work on our part. And the Bible is clear about what that effort entails. But nevertheless, we grow in the grace that only Christ provides. The Christian life, from beginning to end, is ultimately a work of God. Some may believe that we are saved by God's grace, but that our Christian growth is dependent on our works, as if we deserve the credit. That is not true, although Peter does give a command and the Bible does assume that our effort is involved. Because we are so prone to misunderstand this dynamic, Peter reminds us in 2 Peter 3:17 to be on guard. We cannot remain faithful, we cannot guard ourselves, unless God works in us. Our Christian lives are built on grace from beginning to end.

But notice that Peter's last words also command us to grow in knowledge. In our time – when knowledge is so often denigrated and downplayed, when feelings are said to be the determining factor in our worship, when studying the Bible and thinking carefully about doctrine are not even things most churches and most Christians regard as important – we need to hear this message loudly and clearly. The way we avoid being carried away, the way we avoid lawlessness, loss of peace and loss of hope, is by growth in our knowledge of Jesus Christ. This is why, in order to take Peter's command seriously, we need to look continually to Jesus Christ and seek to know him better. We have already seen that this is part of what Peter must mean by growth in grace, and here he makes that claim explicit.

## *Knowledge of Jesus*

Perhaps you have had the experience of meeting someone for the first time. But then imagine that you met someone who knew this person quite well. He or she might say something like, 'Did you know *this*?', 'Did she tell you about *this* experience in her life?', 'Did you know that he studied at *that* university?', 'Did you find out about her early years in *this* city?' And on and on it might go. You would know from these comments that there is more to learn than you possibly imagined. Your knowledge of this person whom you had just met barely begins to plumb the depths of his or her life.

How well do you know Jesus Christ? Do you know him better today than when you first began your Christian life? The apostle Peter, for as well as he knew the Saviour, had not yet plumbed the depths of the person of Jesus Christ. And he realized that the deeper he went, the more he discovered. That is why his last words command us to grow in our knowledge of Jesus Christ. It is the only path to stable and mature Christian living. And if we were to ask Peter how we might go about growing in our knowledge of Christ, he would reply very succinctly: you grow in a knowledge of Jesus by growing in your knowledge of and obedience to his word, the Bible. This is what the Christian life is about; this is the stuff of which Christian growth consists.

All of this, of course, is not merely for us, as if our growth in grace and knowledge was meant for our personal fulfilment or happiness. It may bring that, but it is ultimately for the glory of God. That is why Peter ends with doxology: 'To him be the glory.' The ending is almost identical to that of the Lord's Prayer, though Peter directs his words of glory quite pointedly to Jesus Christ. Peter had followed Jesus for three years, he had denied him three times, and he had seen him raised after three days in the grave. Few were ever closer to Jesus. It was Peter who testified about Jesus throughout the book of Acts. It was Peter who explained the significance of Pentecost. It was he who had to be taught about the equal standing of Jews and Gentiles in the church. Peter now, at the end of his life, stands as a monument to God's grace. He stands as a monument to growth in a knowledge of God and his word. And he quite clearly proclaims, as he had often before, that the man he followed for those years, the one whom he had spent the rest of his life proclaiming as Lord and Saviour, was none other than God himself. It was Jesus, the one true man whom Peter followed, and true God whom he worshipped, who was to receive glory, both now and also in the glorious future when Christ alone will reign.

And so we are commanded: 'Grow in grace, and in the knowledge of the Lord Jesus Christ.'

# 2

# Back to the Beginning
# Ephesians 2:8

*Remembering when*

Sometimes we need to go back to the beginning. We do this all the time. At anniversaries, we go back and remember the day of our wedding or the circumstances of our engagement. We remind our children of their first day of school or the first time they took a step. Sometimes, when we are frustrated with a project, it helps to go back and remember why it was started in the first place.

We may need to go back to the beginning sometimes in our spiritual life as well. When addressing the church in Ephesus in Revelation 2, Jesus instructed the Ephesian church to go back and do just this. To this once great church, Jesus said, 'Consider how far you have fallen! Repent and do the things you did at first …' and 'Remember your first love.'

What about with us? How does going back to the beginning help us to 'grow in grace'? Quite simply, when we go back to the beginning of our Christian lives we see that our beginnings in God's family were an evidence of sheer grace.

### *Grace alone*

Paul writes 'by grace you have been saved'. This is an interesting term – *saved*. When someone is saved they are rescued from something. So the question is, from what have Christians been rescued? Out of what are we saved? Paul has already told us, has he not? There is both a *present* and *future* sense in which we are saved. We are saved from bondage to sin – redeemed by Christ's blood. And we are also saved from the wrath of God. We must be clear about this, because both of these contain present and future elements. The Bible teaches – not least here in Ephesians 2 – that the wrath of God is justly poured out on those who walk in unbelief. But it also teaches that in the future the wrath of God will be poured out on those who have rejected God in Christ. This is where we can begin to talk about a doctrine of hell.

We shy away from this doctrine, but Jesus did not. He talked far more about coming judgment than he did about salvation. Read through the Gospels of Matthew, Mark, Luke, and John and record the occasions when Jesus talked about future judgment. It was a major theme of his preaching and of his ministry in general. So by ignoring it we do a disservice to the Bible itself. How can we overlook or neglect such clear passages. For instance, Revelation 20:11-15:

Then I saw a great white throne and him who was seated on it. From his presence earth and sky fled away, and no place was found for them. And I saw the dead, great and small, standing before the throne, and books were opened. Then another book was opened, which is the book of life. And the dead were judged by what was written in the books, according to what they had done. And the sea gave up the dead who were in it, Death and Hades gave up the dead who were in them, and they were judged, each one of them, according to what they had done. Then Death and Hades were thrown into the lake of fire. This is the second death, the lake of fire. And if anyone's name was not found written in the book of life, he was thrown into the lake of fire.

We ignore these passages at our own peril, and, perhaps most importantly, at the peril of those to whom we are commanded to witness. But I do not bring all this up simply for that reason alone. Unless we reckon with these truths from Scripture, we will not understand the meaning of our salvation at all. If there is no wrath, then there is no need for death. If no one will ever be ultimately and eternally forsaken by God, then why was Jesus forsaken on the cross? When Paul speaks about us being saved, he knows what we have been saved from now, but he also knows what we have been saved from in the future.

So we read that we are rescued by God's grace. But then Paul adds that this comes, 'through faith'. First we must ask what faith is, then what or in whom are we are to believe.

First, what is it faith? This is a difficult question. Theologians have given answers, many of which are very good.

They have stressed the truth that faith is based on facts; it involves the response and commitment of our minds. This is true, though it should be properly qualified. The Bible itself gives a definition of faith in Hebrews 11:1: 'Now faith is the assurance of things hoped for, the conviction of things not seen.' The Bible does not say that faith is a leap in the dark, or a jump into something absurd. In fact, the Bible seems to regard the faithful actions of God's people as the most reasonable thing imaginable. Faith, however, as defined by the author of Hebrews, has to do with something which is yet unseen and also even in the future. One of the most prominent examples of this faith is found in the life of Abraham. In Genesis 22:1-10 we read this story:

> After these things God tested Abraham and said to him, 'Abraham!' And he said, 'Here am I.' He said, 'Take your son, your only son Isaac, whom you love, and go to the land of Moriah, and offer him there as a burnt offering on one of the mountains of which I shall tell you.' So Abraham rose early in the morning, saddled his donkey, and took two of his young men with him, and his son Isaac. And he cut the wood for the burnt offering and arose and went to the place of which God had told him. On the third day Abraham lifted up his eyes and saw the place from afar. Then Abraham said to his young men, 'Stay here with the donkey; I and the boy will go over there and worship and come again to you.' And Abraham took the wood of the burnt offering and laid it on Isaac his son. And he took in his hand the fire and the knife. So they went both of them together. And Isaac said to his father Abraham, 'My father!' And he said, 'Here am I, my son.' He said, 'Behold, the fire

and the wood, but where is the lamb for a burnt offering?' Abraham said, 'God will provide for himself the lamb for a burnt offering, my son.' So they went both of them together.

When they came to the place of which God had told him, Abraham built the altar there and laid the wood in order and bound Isaac his son and laid him on the altar, on top of the wood. Then Abraham reached out his hand and took the knife to slaughter his son.

What do we see here? Abraham did not take a leap into the absurd. He had God's word; he knew of God's power and might; he knew that God was the giver of life. And yet he did not see the way in which God would provide here. He had a command, he had ample evidence that the God who issued the command was powerful and so he acted – perfectly reasonably – in obedient response to that command. Hebrews even tells us that Abraham knew that God was capable of raising someone from the dead. Why should the Creator not be able to give life in that way?

Our faith in respect to salvation looks exactly the same. Think about it. We hear the gospel – the word of God proclaimed. There is abundant evidence for its truthfulness – God raised Jesus from the dead – and yet we are trusting in God for something that we cannot yet see; salvation from sin and eternal life with him. We have abundant convincing evidence of his divine attributes, we know our own sin and we have his word. So, in a sense, the most reasonable thing to do is to obey God's command to repent and trust in Christ alone for salvation. And when we do, by his grace, we are saved.

Paul makes it clear that our salvation is *through* faith – faith is the instrument. But it is *by* God's grace. And, as if to highlight the point, he adds the words at the end of Ephesians 2:8, 'and this not of your own doing; it is the gift of God'. Some have seen this phrase as evidence that even the faith that we have is from God. This is certainly true because we were dead. But, grammatically speaking, this may not be the point Paul is making here, although it may be one implication of it. Paul seems to be saying that our salvation is all a gift from God. It is not something deserved. And the only proper response to a gift of this magnitude is a profound expression of thanks.

So there is a kind of theological problem which Christians often face, attributing salvation to something within themselves. But there is another more prevalent problem facing Christians today. Though we affirm that salvation is a gift from God, we honestly think that if we package Christian teaching in a certain way, people cannot help but be saved. This is exemplified in one of the most popular books on the church published in the last ten years, where the author writes, 'I am convinced that anyone can be won to Christ *if only we can find the key to his or her heart*.' Now that conviction stems from a real and laudable desire to see men and women converted, and certainly we Christians have been too complacent in our evangelism. We are simply afraid to share the gospel with others and we will one day have to answer for that. But, though it stems from good intentions, the statement I quoted undermines what the apostle Paul has written here. If salvation is a gift from God, then not only can we not boast as Christians, but we cannot even boast as evangelists. We are commanded to share the gospel but when God, by his grace, causes someone to believe and be saved, it is his gift, not our prize.

This is the implication of verse 9: 'Not a result of works, so that no one may boast.' Now the implications for us today should be obvious. And all of this is rooted in what the ultimate purpose of our salvation is. We were united with Christ so that God might display the riches of his kindness (Eph. 2:7). It was not for our boasting; our boasting would undermine the gracious nature of the salvation we have been granted.

And I think, specifically, Paul had in mind the claim some were making that their 'works' of keeping the Mosaic law somehow entitled them to salvation on the last day. The reason we know that this is in the back of Paul's mind is that he seems to move seamlessly from a survey of our salvation into a discussion of the Jew-Gentile issue. It was an Old Testament question that had been sharply discussed in the early church. But regardless, we need to keep in mind that no one can boast about salvation, because it is 'not a result of works'.

It is interesting to note that verses 8 and 9 mention 'works' three times. It is worthwhile to consider this. The first use, in verse 8, makes it clear that our salvation is emphatically not of works. But directly on the heels of this assertion comes two more assertions about works. First, Paul writes that we ourselves are God's workmanship. The term used is *poiēma* (the word from which we derive the English word, poem). We are God's work of art, so to speak.

What does this mean? Paul tells us, 'created in Christ Jesus for good works, which God prepared beforehand, that we should walk in them.' Now we see another of the purposes of God's salvation. We were united with Christ in order to show God's mercy and grace, and we have been created in Christ in order to do the good works which God has prepared for us.

We can see here both the essential nature of Christ's work – Christians were chosen *in him*, united *with him*, created *in him* – and we can also see the essential nature of the good works God has for us. We are not our own; we have been bought with a price. So we must not neglect the good works which the Bible commands. In a sense, doing these good things is an essential point of our salvation. If our salvation is designed to bring glory to God, then the good works we do are the specific means of bringing attention to his great glory and grace.

But notice that even when Paul speaks of good works, those too are to be thought of as a result of God's work. They are works which 'God prepared beforehand, that we should walk in them'. This is God's work. We cannot take the credit for it.

Thus we have come full circle. At the beginning of this chapter we saw a picture of ourselves as we were, and humanity as it is. We were dead spiritually, separated from God. And, more than that, we were walking around in sins and transgressions, following Satan himself. Now, after what God has done in us by his grace through our faith, we are no longer condemned to follow the cheap fashions of the world and the devil. Rather we are the workmanship of God, the Master Craftsmen. Instead of walking in futile sins and paralyzing transgressions, we walk now in newness of life. We were created anew in Christ to do good works, which God prepared beforehand, so that *we should walk in them*. What a change! And what grace!

# 3

# A Portrait of Growth
## Hebrews 13:7

Up to this point, we have seen that God commands us to grow in grace and knowledge of the Lord Jesus Christ. To carry this out, we need to go back to the beginning. There we find that our entire Christian experience is one of grace – grace that is given and personified by the person of the Lord Jesus.

But as we begin to grow in grace and knowledge, it will help us if we remember some of those who have gone before us. Each, in his own way, has exemplified aspects of what growing in grace and knowledge looks like in real life. These portraits of growth are intended to show us in a very concrete way what Christian maturity looks like in actual practice. They are valuable resources, given to us by God, and we ought not ignore them.

## *Why study biblical characters?*
Some Christians argue that we ought to avoid studying individual characters in this way. They offer two substantial

reasons which we must address before we go any further. The first objection is essentially a secular one; the second is profoundly Christian.

For the secular mind, biographies present a problem unless – and this is a key caveat – they present their subjects as very flawed people. In this view of biography, we cannot – indeed we should not – elevate one person above another. Everyone is a fraud; no one has anything particular or specific to offer anyone else; all human beings have feet of clay. There is, of course, a sense in which this is true. The Bible teaches that all are sinners, depraved in all their faculties and in utter need of God's kindness and grace. But there is a cynicism at work here as well; one that stems not from a godly humility but from a world-weary despair about life itself and God's ability to accomplish anything through his chosen servants. Nothing is good, nothing matters, no one can or should work hard at anything. Since there is a kernel of truth in this essentially secular view, it may seem persuasive; certainly it is pervasive in our culture today. Many secular biographies are written from this perspective. Even studies of Bible characters (sometimes even of the Lord Jesus Christ himself) are nothing more than debunking efforts, vain attempts to expose the alleged falseness of the Bible's teaching and the hollowness of its leading characters and their beliefs. Ultimately Christians must reject this.

The second objection is more theological and more 'Christian'. This view begins with the truth that anything good that happens in an individual's life is because of God and his grace. Therefore, to pay attention to the human instrument, to attempt to learn anything from them or to emulate them, is to detract from the grace of God. Since it is God's work ultimately, there is no real need to mention the human instruments he has used. This is a serious objection. As Christians, we want no part of praising the creation instead of the Creator. We must not do this.

But this view has two major problems when taken to an extreme. First, it flattens out the work of God – as if everything he accomplishes is done by direct and miraculous means. The fact is that the God who ordains the ends of all things also ordains the means to those ends. God ordained the end of our salvation, but then he also caused us to hear the gospel through the mouth of godly pastors, or parents, or friends. To think about their example and to emulate it, to reflect upon it, is not to detract from the fact that it is God's work. Actually, such reflection helps us to revel in the depth of the riches of his wisdom and grace.

But in addition to this, it seems to me that it is entirely foreign to our common humanity, even as it is expressed in the Bible, to ignore the example of others, supposedly in order to glorify God more fully. Paul tells the church to follow his example (1 Cor. 4:16; 11:1); he says that the Old Testament stories were written as *examples* for our benefit (1 Cor. 10:11; Rom. 13:11). The great cloud of witnesses, whose faith we are to learn from, emulate and consider, are given for our encouragement (Heb. 12:1). Pastors, such as Timothy, are told to be an example to the flock (1 Tim. 4:15); parents are to be an example to their children; older women are to be examples to younger women (Titus 2:3); older men are to be examples of dignity to younger men (Titus 2:2). And on it goes. Those who would tell us never to look at examples for emulation are trying to outsmart and out-spiritualize even the Bible itself. Perhaps the writer to the Hebrews sums it up most succinctly: 'Remember your leaders, those who spoke to you the word of God. *Consider* the outcome of their way of life, and *imitate* their faith' (Heb. 13:7). It is with this in mind that we turn to a biblical portrait of growth in grace and knowledge.

## *A portrait of growth in knowledge*

By any measure Ezra was a remarkable man. The events of his life took place about thirty years before the birth of Plato, though Ezra's ministry was in the land at the opposite end of the Mediterranean Sea. Ezra was known and favoured by the king of Persia, who ruled the known world of that day. In addition, Ezra was a *scribe*. Jewish tradition maintains that Ezra wrote the book (two books in our Bible) of Ezra-Nehemiah; he is said to have also written 1 and 2 Chronicles; some traditions even attribute the collection and organization of the Old Testament canon to Ezra. Beyond that, his organization of the scribes of his day, combined with his own scribal work, led some later Jewish rabbis to refer to him as 'the Second Moses'.

Ezra was also a *preacher*. In Nehemiah 8 we read of a great revival of God's people spurred on by Ezra's preaching of the word of God. He did what all faithful preachers do: he stood up (on a wooden platform, as it happened), opened the book in the sight of everyone, and proclaimed the word of God to a gathering of men, women and children.

Ezra was also a *leader*. We can actually see this in the record of his preaching because, in addition to proclaiming God's word to the people, Ezra organized a team of teachers to go through the crowd afterwards and explain and discuss what had been preached. We could almost say that Ezra oversaw a massive small-group study of the Bible! But his leadership went beyond these instances. In Ezra 7, we read about his leadership of a group of people who left Babylon to travel to Jerusalem by way of Carchemish. This was a dry and difficult journey of between 800 and 900 miles, and he led everyone safely to their destination in three-and-a-half months.

So what made Ezra so successful as a leader and a preacher? Ezra 7:10 explains his success this way: 'For Ezra had set his heart to study the Law of the LORD, and to do it and to teach his statutes and rules in Israel.'

We should note first the description of Ezra's life. He 'set his heart' on three objects. The words used are instructive. Ezra had established or oriented his inner being (the word translated 'heart' can refer to the will, emotions, or thoughts of an individual) in a certain direction. Ezra had set his mind on something; it was fixed; everything was oriented in one direction. We might say that he had dedicated his entire life to a certain pursuit and that anything that did not fit into that pursuit was cast aside as excess baggage. Ezra's mindset was like an athlete in training. He knew that if he fixed his attention on something, there was little room for other pursuits.

And what was the object of Ezra's ambition? According to Ezra 7:10 it was, first, *study* of God's law. Ezra dedicated himself to study the Bible in order to grow in his knowledge of God. It required hard work and meant that lesser tasks had to be put aside. But that is what growth in knowledge demands.

As we look at our own lives, we must consider whether we have this kind of dedication and focus to our study of the Bible. Do you know more about the rules of football than about the minor prophets? Are you more aware of the latest tweet from politicians or celebrities than of the letters of the New Testament? Which books have you read more than the Bible lately? Make no mistake, Ezra grew in the knowledge of God through a focused study of God's word – a study that was a priority in his life. His other areas of success are presented as the overflow of this primary pursuit.

As well as studying the law of God, Ezra dedicated himself to *observing* it. Real growth in knowledge is accompanied by a change in behaviour, because the Bible is a revelation that demands a response from us. Ezra's focus on observance of the law went hand in hand with his study of the law. James reminds us that to merely 'hear' the word and not to 'do' it is a kind of self-deception. It shows that we do not really know what we have just heard. To truly grow in the knowledge of God involves not only the study of God's word, but conscientious obedience to all of its commands.

Now in Ezra's case he was also focused on teaching God's word: 'to teach [the Lord's] statutes and laws in Israel'. Not everyone is called to be a public teacher like Ezra; not everyone should strive to fulfil that kind of role. So at this point we might think that Ezra's example is one from which we may depart. And yet his determination to teach God's word seems to be a part of his pursuit of obedience. He knew what God had called *him* to do and he did *that* with all his might. And surely that is the point we must all grasp here. God calls us to different roles and ministries. But as Paul said to the Colossians: 'Whatever you do, work heartily, as for the Lord and not for men' (Col. 3:23; see also 1 Cor. 10:31; Col. 3:17). Ezra's teaching ministry, then, was just one more way in which he demonstrated his commitment to a full knowledge of God's word, which for him (and for us) involves both deep study and careful practice.

## *Growth in grace*

Perhaps we will not be surprised to see that Ezra's growth in true biblical knowledge was actually a visible outworking of his growth in grace. As we have seen, Ezra's success is attributed to his dedicated pursuit of a knowledge of God's word (7:10). But when Ezra reflects on his successes later in the same chapter, he attributes everything to the grace of the Lord. He says this:

> Blessed be the Lord, the God of our fathers, who put such a thing as this into the heart of the king, to beautify the house of the Lord that is in Jerusalem, and who extended to me his steadfast love before the king and his counsellors,

and before all the king's mighty officers. I took courage, for the hand of the Lord my God was on me, and I gathered leading men from Israel to go up with me (7:27-28).

Two phrases should strike us when we read this. The first is 'his steadfast love'; the second, 'the hand of the Lord my God'. The first – *his steadfast love* – is of the utmost significance in the Old Testament. 'Steadfast love' is a translation of the Hebrew word *hesed* which refers to God's covenant faithfulness and grace to his people. In other words, when Ezra looks at his accomplishments, he sees them as an outworking of the saving and preserving grace of God.

The second – *the hand of the Lord my God* – is a phrase that Ezra frequently employs. It is his way of showing, once again, that everything that happens in his life comes as a result of God's gracious provision. Ezra uses this phrase in 7:6; 8:18, 22, 31 and in Nehemiah 2:8. It becomes one of his favourite ways of describing the blessing of God upon his life. Ezra's understanding of life is echoed by the apostle Paul. For instance, in 1 Corinthians 15:10, Paul writes,

> But by the grace of God I am what I am, and his grace toward me was not in vain. On the contrary, I worked harder than any of them, though it was not I, but the grace of God that is with me.

Growing in knowledge is hard work. The study of the Bible demands the best of our faculties and the best of our time. And as we grow in knowledge, by both studying and doing, God is at work to cause us to grow in grace.

# PART 2

# THE ADVENT OF GRACE

# 4

# Our Prophet Who Teaches
# Hebrews 1:1, 2

*A better prophet*

Who was the best teacher you ever had? Perhaps it was someone who taught a subject you loved, or coached you in a sport you enjoyed playing. Maybe your best teacher actually taught something you did not naturally appreciate; teachers like that 'win us over' with their infectious zeal.

Good teachers play a significant role in our growth as Christians. This is why Christian pastors are commanded to study, to teach and preach – and to train others to teach as well (2 Tim. 2:2). The best teachers are students of God's word, like Ezra. In looking at Ezra, we saw a portrait of a student of God's word. Ezra was a man whose life was oriented around studying, obeying, and teaching the Scriptures. He was blessed by God for this. The Lord used Ezra to lead in ways that were far-reaching and profound.

Beyond just being a student of God's word, Ezra was also a prophet of God. What does it mean to be God's prophet?

In Exodus 7:1, 2, the LORD gives Moses and Aaron the task of speaking to Pharaoh. As each of their roles is defined, God commands Aaron to act as the 'prophet' of Moses. What this means is clearly spelled out to Moses: 'You shall speak all that I command you, and your brother Aaron shall speak to Pharaoh that he let the sons of Israel go out of his land' (Exod. 7:2). The position of 'prophet' was simple: the prophet heard what was said to him (in this case, by Moses) and then he, in turn, proclaimed that message to its intended audience. Because prophets of God were his intended mouthpiece to the people, hearers had to be on guard. If the prophet ever said something that did not come to pass, he would have to be stoned (Deut. 18:21, 22); and even if what he said came true, the rest of his message needed to be tested against the teaching of Scripture (Deut. 13:1-5). Prophets like Ezra were teachers and mouthpieces of God to his people. So when someone claimed to have a word from God, that word had to be held up to close scrutiny. But the true prophets – the ones who really were speaking God's word – were responsible for the Old Testament Scriptures, as they were guided and governed by the Holy Spirit himself. As Peter puts it: 'knowing this first of all, that no prophecy of Scripture comes from someone's own interpretation. For no prophecy was ever produced by the will of man, but men spoke from God as they were carried along by the Holy Spirit' (2 Pet. 1:20, 21).

Imagine what the situation of the believers in the Old Testament would have been without the ministry of the prophets. They would have had no clarity regarding the will of God for their lives. They would not have had the wonderful ministry of correction in which the prophets made their sins clear and their path to repentance plain. Again and again, God sent prophets to his people. Most of the time they were rejected. But for those with ears to hear, their message was life-giving and spiritually sustaining.

Even as great as those prophets were – men like Moses, Elijah, and Ezra – we have a better prophet today. As much as Ezra devoted himself to study and obey and teach, we have a more learned, obedient, and gifted teacher. Ezra was led by the Holy Spirit to speak and write the word of God. Our prophet is the Word made flesh. As the writer to the Hebrews puts it: 'Long ago, at many times and in many ways, God spoke to our fathers by the prophets, but in these last days he has spoken to us by his Son, whom he appointed the heir of all things, through whom also he created the world' (Heb. 1:1, 2).

In this short opening statement, the writer to the Hebrews identifies three ways in which the teaching ministry of Jesus is superior to that of the Old Testament prophets. First, Jesus' ministry is 'in these last days'; second, the Son, unlike the prophets, is the heir of all things; third, the Son is the creator of the world, not merely a creature within the world.

### A prophet for the last days
Jesus' ministry as the spokesman for God is a ministry for, 'these last days.' This is a phrase that appears several times in the New Testament. It is given as a contrast to the period

of the Old Testament, before the coming of the Lord Jesus Christ. It is not an easy time. In fact, the apostle Paul has this to say about the last days:

> But understand this, that in the last days there will come times of difficulty. For people will be lovers of self, lovers of money, proud, arrogant, abusive, disobedient to their parents, ungrateful, unholy, heartless, unappeasable, slanderous, without self-control, brutal, not loving good, treacherous, reckless, swollen with conceit, lovers of pleasure rather than lovers of God, having the appearance of godliness, but denying its power (2 Tim. 3:1-5a).

To be sure, the last days are difficult days for Christians. In fact, what becomes clear when reading the remainder of Paul's words is that the most destructive and sinful aspects of the last days happen within the church, not just in the world. But despite the difficulties, despite the hypocrisy and sin, living in these last days means that we have the revelation of God's only Son, Jesus Christ. He is the prophet of the last day, predicted in the Old Testament but realized by we who live in these times (see especially Acts 3:19-23).

Not only is this a comfort, but it also serves as a reminder that no future prophet is necessary. There would be no greater revelation of God to come by another prophet. Many major religions acknowledge the revelation of Jesus, but then go on to suggest that his revelation is made more complete by yet another latter prophet. Jesus is the prophet given to us for the difficult last days before his return. No other prophet will surpass him, and it is his word alone that we need.

## *A prophet who is heir of all things*

But Jesus is not only the prophet for our own day, he is also the one in whom all authority is vested; indeed, as Hebrews tells us, he is 'appointed heir of all things.' This means that in addition to being the best of all teachers, he is also the one who is sovereign over everything. This makes an immense difference, especially when it comes to the promises given by Jesus.

The Old Testament prophets, great as they were, did not have the power to effect the events they described. If they were genuine prophets and they promised judgement or blessing, then it would surely come to pass. God would see to it. But, while the prophets could make certain promises, they were not directly responsible for the fulfilment of those promises. But Jesus, the greater prophet, is both entirely reliable in his promises, *and is the one who will be responsible for bringing them to pass.*

No one expected this from the Old Testament prophets. Just because they promised that God would do something, no one required them to make it happen. And similarly, one of the marks of the true prophet (according to Deut. 13) is that they pointed people's worship and attention to God alone – not to themselves, not to other kings, leaders or idols.

Jesus was entirely different. Not only did he promise great things, he said that he would be the one to deliver them! He directed his hearers' attention and worship to himself. We have examples of this in the gospels and they are among the most precious promises of Scripture. In John 6, Jesus promises eternal life to those who come to him in faith. But he does not merely state this in an abstract way. Instead he says, 'whoever comes to me I will not cast out' (John 6:36b). Similarly, Jesus affirms that, 'Everyone who has heard and learned from the Father comes to me' (John 6:45b). Jesus is unlike any other prophets in that his prophetic message finds its terminus in him. In the case of future events, like the resurrection and the judgment, he will see to their fulfilment. And his hearers' trust, attention, and worship should be focused on him alone.

### A prophet who is the creator

One of the most moving prophetic passages in the Old Testament is Isaiah 40. The prophet Isaiah comforts the people of Israel by reminding them of God's mighty power as creator. Speaking as God's mouthpiece, he ends his message in this way:

> To whom then will you compare me, that I should be like him? says the Holy One. Lift up your eyes on high and see: who created these? He who brings out their host by number, calling them all by name; by the greatness of his might and because he is strong in power, not one is missing. Why do you say, O Jacob, and speak, O Israel, "My way is hidden from the LORD, and my right is disregarded by my God"? Have you not known? Have you not heard? The LORD is the everlasting God, the Creator of the ends of the earth. He does not faint or grow weary; his understanding is unsearchable. He gives power to the faint, and to him

who has no might he increases strength. Even youths shall faint and be weary, and young men shall fall exhausted; but they who wait for the LORD shall renew their strength; they shall mount up with wings like eagles; they shall run and not be weary; they shall walk and not faint (Isa. 40:25-31).

The connection that Isaiah draws is quite straightforward. Because God is the creator, he is without peer and beyond comparing. Because God is the creator, nothing escapes his notice and nothing can be hidden from him. Because God is the creator, he is able to give strength to those who need it most.

But what if the prophet himself was this Creator God? What if the one bearing the message was also the one who gave life to the recipients? This is exactly what Hebrews says is true about Jesus our final prophet. He is the one who can do what the LORD was said to do in Isaiah's day. In fact, he is the LORD incarnate. So as we listen to the words of Jesus, we can know that he knows us entirely, and he can sustain us by his Spirit as we follow his word.

## Conclusion

Because we are creatures and are prone to wander, we need a message (a revelation) from God. We need to be taught who he is, what he requires, what he has provided. People have always needed a prophet.

When we look at the Old Testament we see God graciously providing for his people in this way. Abel, Noah, Moses, Elijah, Isaiah, Jonah, Daniel and many others were given for just this task. In his kindness, God revealed himself through these men, and in many cases preserved their revelation so that we could learn from it even today.

But today we have so much more. Not only do we have the prophets of the Old Testament, but we have the true and final prophet of whom they spoke. He is the ultimate teacher, of course, but he also gives us the word which is sufficient for these last days of difficulty. We have the prophet who not only speaks but also has acted and will act decisively to bring about all that he has spoken. And we have the prophet who is our creator. He knows all things; he is worthy of our worship; and he can sustain us as his creatures. Once again, we see God's great provision for us. And once again, we are reminded about how closely we must cling to the revelation he has given. This prophet – our teacher – trains and equips us to grow in our Christian lives.

# 5

# Our Priest Who Intercedes
# Hebrews 8:1, 2

### *What is a priest?*

In our modern culture many people grow up without any contact with a priest. Perhaps when you hear the word 'priest' you think of the man who leads the Roman Catholic Church in your city or town. For many in our culture, this is the only mental picture that comes to mind when the priesthood is mentioned.

The ancient world, however, was full of priests. The priest was the human mediator between a pagan god and the human worshippers of that god. In the Old Testament, the Lord himself had priests. They were ordained for two major tasks. First, they were teachers – scattered throughout the Promised Land, carefully guiding people in their understanding of the Scriptures. But second, these priests were charged with keeping up the sacrifices and offerings – first in the tabernacle, then later in the Jerusalem temple. The priests of Israel were all to come from the tribe of Levi.

This dual identity – part of a tribe and pursuing a priestly vocation – meant that sometimes the Bible used the terms almost interchangeably: Levites were known primarily for their role as priests, and all priests had to be Levites.

Both the teaching and sacrificial aspects were important, but of the two, the average priest would spend far more of his time teaching. There were only so many Levitical priests necessary to keep up the sacrifices of the tabernacle and the temple, and many of the priests operated on a kind of rotating basis.[1] So for most of their lives, the vast majority of Levites settled throughout the land of Israel, serving in the name of the Lord, teaching and counselling believers who sought to live according to God's word. They were supported by the people and they had no permanent inheritance in the Promised Land. Deuteronomy 18 outlines this arrangement and gives us a picture of what the normal life of a Levite might be like:

> The Levitical priests, all the tribe of Levi, shall have no portion or inheritance with Israel. They shall eat the Lord's food offerings as their inheritance. They shall have no inheritance among their brothers; the Lord is their inheritance, as he promised them ... And if a Levite comes from any of your towns out of all Israel, where he lives – and he may come when he desires – to the place that the Lord will choose, and ministers in the name of the Lord his God, like all his fellow Levites who stand to minister there before the Lord, then he may have equal

[1] See, for instance, Luke 1:8, 9 for how this operated in the first century AD.

portions to eat, besides what he receives from the sale of his patrimony (Deut. 18:1, 2, 6-8).

This was a gracious provision of God for his people. But the priests were human beings with limitations and failings. Like any human teacher or counsellor, they did not always understand or relate to the people for whom they were to care. We have an example of this in 1 Samuel 1. There we read of a godly woman named Hannah. Hannah was embarrassed by her husband and his other wife and she was bereft of a child. She was deeply humiliated and regularly provoked for this. And yet year after year Hannah faithfully prayed to the Lord. She trusted God with her pain and she pleaded with him for deliverance and blessing.

On one such occasion, as she humbly prayed and wept in the temple, the high priest noticed her. But instead of consoling her, he misjudged her completely. We read, 'Hannah was speaking in her heart; only her lips moved, and her voice was not heard. Therefore Eli took her to be a drunken woman. And Eli said to her, "How long will you go on being drunk? Put your wine away from you"' (1 Sam. 1:13, 14). Instead of sensitivity, Hannah received a rebuke! When she needed comfort, she got only the cold condemnation of a religious leader.

In this case, Eli was not intending to be insensitive. As soon as Hannah explained the situation, he responded with care and a blessing. But like all human comforters, he did not immediately and instinctively respond as he should have. His knowledge and experience was incomplete. He

41

did not know what Hannah was enduring, and he mistook her godly actions for sinful ones. Even priests seeking to counsel and teach with the best of intentions could get it wrong. After all, they were merely human teachers and counsellors.

In addition to their teaching and counselling role, the Levitical priests served in the tabernacle and later in the temple. There they were responsible for handling the offerings and sacrifices of the people. This was certainly their most visible role, and it required special purification and cleansing in preparation.

We see the first ordination ceremony in Leviticus 8. In addition to the oil that was used for the consecration of the priests, and the special clothing that they were commanded to wear, both a bull and a ram were killed and then burned as part of the ceremony. The ram was for a sweet savoury offering to the Lord – essentially a way of offering visible and costly thanks to God – but the bull was for sin. These priests, though specially consecrated by the Lord for special service, were sinners.

Their sinful status was underscored in two dramatic chapter in Leviticus. The first of these is the account of the high holy day called *Yom Kippur* or, in English, the Day of Atonement. On this day and only on this day, the high priest would enter the holiest place in the temple. He would bring blood with him, first for his own sins, then for the sins of the people. On this most solemn day, the priests and the people were all reminded of something about their sacrificial system: even the priests approached God as sinners.

As a chilling reminder of this, Leviticus 10 narrates another story in the life of the tabernacle. This came, strangely enough, on the very first day it was constructed. The tabernacle had just been completed and the first priests were ordained for its service. These first two priests were sons of Aaron himself, the nephews of Moses, and their names were Nadab and Abihu. As Nadab and Abihu went in on the very first day, we read this: 'Now Nadab and Abihu, the sons of Aaron, each took his censer and put fire in it and laid incense on it and offered unauthorized fire before the LORD, which he had not commanded them.[2] And fire came out from before the LORD and consumed them, and they died before the LORD' (Lev. 10:1, 2). Imagine the scene. This is the first day of the tabernacle. God has made a way to visibly travel with his people. He has given them gracious instructions for how to approach him in thanksgiving. He has set up a priesthood that can present sin offerings on their behalf. And yet there is an obvious weakness in the system. The priests themselves are sinners. At their very best, they needed to present offerings for themselves first; at their worst, their own disobedience actually impeded worship altogether. From the first day of the ministry of these earthly priests, it became clear that a better, more sure priest was needed. There was an inherent instability to the tabernacle and the temple because it was run by flawed and sinful people. Just as the Levites were often insensitive and prone to mistakes in their teaching, so especially in their work in the tabernacle their human frailty was on vivid display. And then, for the very best priests, there was always the reality of death. Even if they served well, their service would one day end. After all, they were only human.

## A sympathetic priest

So the priestly system in Israel was good but flawed. The flaws had nothing to do with the way the system was designed, but had everything to do with how it was executed by the human priests. The best priests would have been humble and helpful teachers, but when they approached the temple they would have been reminded of their sin. And they probably would have been reminded of their sin at other points as well, as they struggled to understand and care for the people entrusted to them.

But Jesus' priesthood is entirely different. He suffered beyond what any mere human can imagine. In his humanity he experienced rejection, loss, abandonment, physical and emotional pain. He is fully able to sympathize with all who come to him. He knew temptation and in fact endured it far more comprehensively than anyone ever could, since he resisted it fully at every step. Here is the way Hebrews puts it: 'For we do not have a high priest who is unable to sympathize with our weaknesses, but one who in every respect has been tempted as we are, yet without sin. Let us then with confidence draw near to the throne of grace, that we may receive mercy and find grace to help in time of need' (Heb. 4:15, 16).

Do you see the implications of this? In an Old Testament context, there might be reason for hesitation when coming to a priest for help. Could he really understand? Would he possess any sympathy? Could he possibly relate to all our struggles? Will he take advantage of us or manipulate in a sinful way? These would be relevant questions with a merely human priest, but with Jesus we can and must draw near confidently. He is a sympathetic high priest, who has endured all temptations and can be relied upon since he is without sin.

## *A holy priest*

This teaching about Jesus being without sin has implications that reach far beyond his role as a counsellor and helper. They also inform our understanding of his role as our mediator before God. Remember that Old Testament priests, even at their best, had to offer sacrifices for themselves first. Then, after offering these sacrifices to address their own sinful state, they could begin to offer the sacrifices of the people. This weakness was inherent in the system. If you brought your sacrifice before the Lord in good faith, you could never quite be certain of the status of the priest. Some priests actively undermined the sacrificial system and used it for their own selfish gain. Some, like Nadab and Abihu, were at least careless in following the commands. All of them were sinners in need of their own atonement. And even the best of them would die.

But Hebrews writes this about Jesus' work as our high priest:

> The former priests were many in number, because they were prevented by death from continuing in office, but he

holds his priesthood permanently, because he continues forever. Consequently, he is able to save to the uttermost those who draw near to God through him, since he always lives to make intercession for them. For it was indeed fitting that we should have such a high priest, holy, innocent, unstained, separated from sinners, and exalted above the heavens. He has no need, like those high priests, to offer sacrifices daily, first for his own sins and then for those of the people, since he did this once for all when he offered up himself. For the law appoints men in their weakness as high priests, but the word of the oath, which came later than the law, appoints a Son who has been made perfect forever (Heb. 7:23-28).

What a remarkable picture! Jesus, the sympathetic high priest, is also the perfect and eternal one. He does not have to offer sacrifices for his own sin – he was without sin. And the sacrifice he did offer was perfect and 'once for all.' In addition to his strength and perfection, he lives eternally. You will never approach Jesus and find that he is no longer there or that his priestly service has ended. It is reliable, steadfast, and eternal.

And the sacrifice Jesus offers is far greater than the sacrifice of a bull or goat, which could never fully cleanse the conscience. No – Jesus' 'once for all' sacrifice is his very self. He is both priest and sacrifice. His work enables those who trust in him to have assurance before God and hope for the future. This makes us ready to serve with openness and gladness, and to obey with poise and confidence. For indeed, as Hebrews reminds us: 'For if the sprinkling of defiled persons with the blood of goats and bulls and with the ashes of a heifer sanctifies for the purification of the flesh, how much more will the blood of Christ, who through the eternal Spirit offered himself without blemish to God, purify our conscience from dead works to serve the living God' (Heb. 9:13, 14).

# 6

# Our King Who Leads
## Matthew 21:5

*Ancient kings*

For most of us living in the modern West, kings are a charming anachronism. They seem to come from a bygone age or a fairy tale. Many still enjoy following the ceremonies of the British royal family, or the news and pictures that occasionally come from one of the other formerly great kingdoms of Europe. But even for those who live in nations or provinces which have a king or queen, the actual effect of that monarch on the life of an average citizen is more ceremonial than anything else. Kings and queens today are viewed as symbols at most; in many cases, they are hardly seen as more than particularly exotic celebrities.

But of course this was not at all true in the ancient world. In times past, kings and queens held great sway over the affairs of ordinary people. Their word was law and they were nearly always viewed as the living embodiment of the kingdom itself. In many ancient kingdoms, the king was viewed as an actual god, someone far greater than a mere human being. This may be one of the reasons why the Lord condemned the people of Israel for their demand to have a king in 1 Samuel 8. There we read: 'And the LORD said to Samuel, "Obey the voice of the people in all they say to you, for they have not rejected you, but they have rejected me from being king over them"' (verse 7). The Lord knew that behind the desire of the Israelites to have a king was a deeper desire to throw off the authority of God and to resemble the pagan nations surrounding them.

## *A king in Israel*

But the idea of a king in Israel was not always portrayed in negative terms. In Genesis 17 God expands upon his glorious covenant promise to Abraham, saying 'I will make you exceedingly fruitful, and I will make you into nations, and kings shall come from you' (Gen. 17:6). Later on in the book of Genesis, when Jacob is blessing his sons (from whom would come the tribes of Israel), he declares this about one of his sons, Judah: 'The sceptre shall not depart from Judah, nor the ruler's staff from between his feet, until tribute comes to him; and to him shall be the obedience of the peoples' (Gen. 49:10). Even in the law that God gives to the people at Mt Sinai, a king is anticipated. This king had certain restrictions placed upon him, and if he was to be a faithful king, he would need to give himself entirely in obedience to God.[1] But the point is that a king

---

[1] See Deut. 17:14-20 for more detail on the guidelines for an Israelite king.

in Israel – especially the promised king from the line of Judah – was not an inherently bad thing. In fact, there is a repeated refrain in the book of Judges, 'In those days there was no king in Israel. Everyone did what was right in his own eyes.' This statement *no king in Israel* was a way of summarizing and explaining the moral and political chaos in the land. The Israelites needed a king but they needed the right kind of king – the promised one, whom God had chosen.

Israel's first experience of a king was a failure. They chose the king for all the wrong reasons and his heart was not fully devoted to the Lord. But Israel's second king, David, was very different. He was chosen by God and blessed by God's hand. After David's kingdom was consolidated, he wanted to build a permanent temple in Jerusalem for the Lord. But after consulting with the prophet Nathan, about this plan, David received a different message from the Lord. In essence, the Lord told David that he would not build a house for the Lord (the temple in Jerusalem), but that the Lord would instead build David's house and establish his kingdom. God's promise to David culminates with these words: 'And your house and your kingdom shall be made sure forever before me. Your throne shall be established forever' (2 Sam. 7:16).

As the story of Israel progresses in the Old Testament, kings come and go and none of them ever lives up to the ideals of Deuteronomy, nor do any fit the description of the king who would sit on the throne of David forever. But during Israel's time of exile, this promise is still held out.

The prophets remind the people of it regularly. In one special prophecy, the Lord speaks through the prophet Ezekiel about the future work of restoration and renewal: 'And I will make them one nation in the land, on the mountains of Israel. And one king shall be over them all' (Ezek. 37:22a). And again: 'My servant David shall be king over them, and they shall all have one shepherd. They shall walk in my rules and be careful to obey my statutes' (Ezek. 37:24). The glorious promise at the end of the Old Testament is that God was still planning to send the long-awaited king and not only would that king follow God's rules and statutes, but the people of that king would do the same.

## King Jesus

It is nearly impossible for any of us to imagine the questions and emotions that Mary must have experienced when the angel announced that she would conceive a baby by the Holy Spirit. At the very least there must have been a strange combination of anxiety and wonder in her mind. But apart from the miracle itself, the identity of the child must have astonished her. After identifying the Lord's blessing on her the angel has these words about the baby: 'He will be great and will be called the Son of the Most High. And the Lord God will give to him the throne of his father David, and he will reign over the house of Jacob forever, and of his kingdom there will be no end' (Luke 1:32, 33). This royal birth is not only connected to David by the angel but in Mary's song of praise, and later in the poetic prophesy of Zechariah the priest, the promise of this Davidic king is tied to the promises God initially made to Abraham (see Luke 1:55 and 1:73-75). God was fulfilling the ancient promise of a king through the birth of Jesus.

But it is not simply faithful Jews such as Mary and Zechariah who understand these truths about Jesus. In the Gospel of Matthew we see the Gentile wise men approach Jesus as a king. They travel from a great distance, seeking out Jesus as the one born 'king of the Jews.' Their journey is guided by a quotation from the prophet Micah in reference to the one who would be the king and shepherd of Israel (see Matt. 2:1-7). When they arrive, they offer gifts of tribute and worship Jesus joyfully.

The Gospel of Mark, which does not recount the birth and early years of Jesus, nonetheless emphasizes Jesus' kingship. Mark does this by using the kingly word *authority* to describe what Jesus does and says. In Mark 1, for instance, Jesus is shown to be a teacher with unusual power – even over demons. After casting out a demon, the people respond: 'What is this? A new teaching with authority! He commands even the unclean spirits and they obey him' (Mark 1:27b). Jesus then goes on to show authority over disease, sin, and creation itself.[1] Truly, he is the powerful Lord and king promised in the Old Testament.

### Not that kind of king

In light of this, perhaps the most surprising fact about Jesus' behaviour as king is the way in which he exercises this absolute authority. In one important encounter with

---

[1] See for instance, Mark 2:1-12, and Mark 4:35-41.

his disciples, as they begin to grasp who he is as their king, two of the disciples request to sit at Jesus' right hand and left hand in his glory. He responds by explaining once again his coming crucifixion, but he also redefines 'authority' and the way in which it must be exercised among Christians:

> Jesus called them to him and said to them, 'You know that those who are considered rulers of the Gentiles lord it over them, and their great ones exercise authority over them. But it shall not be so among you. But whoever would be great among you must be your servant, and whoever would be first among you must be slave of all. For even the Son of Man came not to be served but to serve, and to give his life a ransom for many' (Mark 10:42-45).

The astonishing reality of Jesus' kingship is that, despite his absolute authority, he demonstrates his kingly reign primarily through suffering service. This is what lies behind his quotation from the prophet Zechariah as he was entering Jerusalem at the beginning of the week in which he was to be crucified, the event that Christians call the Triumphal Entry on Palm Sunday. In a quotation that seems far removed from our general understanding of triumph and victory, Jesus cites this Old Testament passage: 'Say to the daughter of Zion, "Behold, your king is coming to you, humble, and mounted on a donkey, and on a colt, the foal of a beast of burden"' (Matt. 21:5, quoting Zech. 9:9).

## The triumph of the king

What does the kingship of Jesus have to do with Christians growing in grace today? Perhaps the major implications could be summarized with three terms: confidence, clarity and redefinition.

First, *confidence*. Because Jesus is king, this means that he is the one with all authority. In fact, this is the very note Jesus himself strikes in his great commission to the disciples: 'All authority in heaven and on earth has been given to me' (Matt. 28:18). This is the foundation for his command to 'go and make disciples,' to 'baptize,' 'teaching them to observe all that I have commanded. …'[1] We must remember that this commission is not given to those who were entirely convinced of Jesus' power. Here is how the disciples are described in the verse just before the commission is given: 'And when they saw him they worshipped him, but some doubted' (Matt. 28:17). This worship-mixed-with-doubt is the background for Jesus' declaration that he possessed all authority. We need to be reminded of the kingship of Jesus over all things precisely when we doubt. In Question 26 of the Westminster Shorter Catechism, this is the implication of Christ's kingship that is described:

> Q. 26. *How doth Christ execute the office of a king?*
> A. Christ executeth the office of a king, in subduing us to himself, in ruling and defending us, and in restraining and conquering all his and our enemies.[2]

[1] This entire commission is found in Matthew 28:18-20.
[2] The Westminster Shorter Catechism is a question and answer document, originally written in the seventeenth century, which overviews

Christ is our conquering king. His final defeat of sin, Satan and his enemies will be effected at the end of human history, but his authority is certain even now.[1] This should give us confidence as we serve him in the midst of trials today.

But the kingship of Jesus should also bring great *clarity* to our lives. Who is it that we ought to obey? How should we live our lives? In one important sense the answer is clear and simple: we should obey those to whom Jesus has delegated authority, and we should live our lives according to the commands King Jesus has given. In the world, this means we submit to governing authorities instituted by God (Rom. 13:1). In the church, Jesus has given elders to shepherd and oversee his church (1 Pet. 5:2). In every area of our lives the Bible – given by God through the prophets and apostles – is to be our rule and guidebook. The scriptures provide the marching orders of our king. It is through the preaching of this word that Christ leads and speaks to us today.

And finally, the kingship of Jesus *redefines* the way in which authority is to be exercised among us as Christians. Jesus makes it clear that true greatness in his kingdom consists of humble service to others. This is why Jesus quotes from Zechariah even as he is entering Jerusalem to lay

---

biblical doctrine. The Shorter Catechism is available from the Trust as a small booklet or combined in a large clothbound volume with the Confession of Faith, the Larger Catechism, and other historical documents associated with the Westminster Assembly.

[1] For a description of the final victory and judgment, see Rev. 21:7-15.

down his life. To be a humble servant is to have the mind of King Jesus. As Paul writes about his great heavenly king:

> Do nothing from rivalry or conceit, but in humility count others more significant than yourselves. Let each of you look not only to his own interests, but also to the interests of others. Have this mind among yourselves, which is yours in Christ Jesus, who, though he was in the form of God, did not count equality with God a thing to be grasped, but made himself nothing, taking the form of a servant, being born in the likeness of men. And being found in human form, he humbled himself by becoming obedient to the point of death, even death on a cross. Therefore God has highly exalted him and bestowed on him the name that is above every name, so that at the name of Jesus every knee should bow, in heaven and on earth and under the earth, and every tongue confess that Jesus Christ is Lord, to the glory of God the Father (Phil. 2:3-11).

# PART 3

# THE MEANS OF GRACE

# 7

# The House that Jesus Builds
# Matthew 16:18

### *A place to grow*

Christians are meant to grow in a community. Just as children benefit from a stable home, Christians grow in grace within the context of the church. In fact this is so integral to the Christian life that the New Testament does not envision any other kind of Christian life at all. As the gospel was spreading rapidly in the early decades of the church, there were certainly new believers who did not immediately have a church home. But it is striking to note that they are never left in that condition. The apostle Paul in Acts does not simply share the gospel in order to see individual converts, he obeys the Lord's command to make disciples and ultimately to plant churches. We see this repeatedly in the book of Acts, but we also see it very strikingly presented in his little letter to Titus. Having worked together with Titus on the island of Crete and having seen many conversions, Paul recognized that the work was unfinished.

He left Titus to organize congregations: 'This is why I left you in Crete, so that you might put what remained into order, and appoint elders in every town as I directed you' (Titus 1:5). It is clear as the letter progresses that Christians at every stage – from those who have just been converted to those who are mature in every way – must be part of a Christian congregation. Paul grounds this involvement in the fact that we have been exploring up to this point in our book: 'For the grace of God has appeared (Titus 2:11).'[1]

We can see this corporate focus in Paul's other letters as well. For instance, in his letter to the Ephesians Paul outlines the gospel of God's grace in the first three chapters, beginning with predestination. He mentions the eternal purposes of God, the adoption which Christians enjoy into God's family, the unity we have in Christ, the nature of salvation – all of grace. He explains his own ministry as a servant of this gospel. Then, after surveying these biblical truths, he commands individual Christians to 'walk in a manner worthy of the calling to which you have been called' (Eph. 4:1). Interestingly, Paul does not describe this 'worthy walk' in the way we normally might. He does not say that the worthy walk involves individual acts of piety or devotion. Rather, the 'worthy walk' is all focused on others: 'with all humility and patience, bearing with one another in love, eager to maintain the unity of the Spirit in the bond of peace' (Eph. 4:2, 3). In other

---

[1] In Titus 2:1-10, Paul explains the roles that individuals at different stages are to play in one another's lives.

words, Christians work out their calling in the gospel in community with others. Just as people grow in families, Christians grow in the church.[1]

## *A covenant community*

The church is a special kind of institution. It is a community grounded in a covenant. This is most clearly seen in the two sacraments ordained for the church by the Lord Jesus Christ, baptism and communion. Although there are debates among Bible-believing Christians about the proper subjects of baptism, all agree that it is a sign instituted by God that speaks of his covenant love and forgiveness. Similarly the Lord's Supper, as we have already seen, points us to a covenant as well. The words Jesus used to describe the drinking of the cup make this very clear: 'This cup is the new covenant in my blood… '[2]

This aspect of the church is important for us to understand. Covenants may seem a bit archaic to us today, but they played a significant role in the ancient world and they are near the vital centre of what God reveals about himself and his people in the Bible.[3] There are many facets to this truth but, simply put, the fact that the church is a covenant community reminds us, first, that it is a community based upon God's promises. The word of Jesus Christ is what

[1] For an excellent introduction to the church that goes beyond what is covered in this chapter, see Mark G. Johnston, *The Church: Glorious Body, Radiant Bride* (Edinburgh: Banner of Truth Trust, 2018).

[2] Quoted in 1 Cor. 11:25.

[3] For a clear introduction to these concepts, see Jonty Rhodes, *Covenants Made Simple* (Phillipsburg, NJ: P & R, 2013).

binds together the church. Jesus is the ruler of the church and his promises are what we are all partakers of. Paul's words make this clear:

> When you read this, you can perceive my insight into the mystery of Christ, which was not made known to the sons of men in other generations as it has now been revealed to his holy apostles and prophets by the Spirit. This mystery is that the Gentiles are fellow heirs, members of the same body, and partakers of the promise in Jesus Christ through the gospel (Eph. 4:4-6).

In the past, God's people had been divided in various ways, most notably between Jews and Gentiles. But the church is described as one body, with all the members united by the promise in Jesus Christ.

And since we are all partakers of Christ's promise, we are bound together as one body. Paul discusses this metaphor at length in his letter to the Corinthian church. It is worth reading in full, but two excerpts will make it clear how important this understanding of the church is:

> For just as the body is one and has many members, and all the members of the body, though many, are one body, so it is with Christ. For in one Spirit we were all baptized into one body – Jews or Greeks, slaves or free – and all were made to drink of one Spirit … Now you are the body of Christ and individually members of it (1 Cor. 12:12, 13, 27).

Perhaps the most dramatic moment in which this truth was driven home was the conversion of Paul himself. Paul (who was known as Saul at that time) was viciously persecuting the church. His threats and murders made it unsafe for many Christians in Jerusalem, so he planned to travel north to Damascus to execute the same strategy against the Christians living there. While on his way to Damascus, Jesus appeared to him. Jesus' words are worth pondering. Here is the account: 'And falling to the ground he [Saul] heard a voice saying to him, "Saul, Saul, why are you persecuting me?" And he said, "Who are you, Lord?" And he said, "I am Jesus, whom you are persecuting."'

Notice that Saul was attacking the church, but Jesus referred to it as 'persecuting me.' The implication could not be clearer. The church is the body of Christ. It is so closely identified with Jesus that to persecute the church is to persecute him. God's covenant mediated through Jesus Christ is what the church is all about. We are members of a body, working together under the terms of God's covenant to his people.

## *A worshipping community*

One of the first things we see take place when the Holy Spirit descends at Pentecost is believers gathering to worship together. In the book of Acts, we see the church devoting itself to four specific things. Luke writes, 'And they devoted themselves to the apostles' teaching, and the fellowship, to the breaking of bread, and the prayers' (Acts 2:42). Later, in 1 Timothy, Paul gives a basic outline of some elements in this public worship. He mentions public prayer, reading Scripture, exhortation, and preaching (1 Tim. 2:1; 4:13). Elsewhere we read of singing (especially psalms), giving financially, and participating in the Lord's Supper (Eph. 5:19; 2 Cor. 9:7; 1 Cor. 11:23-26).

It is so gracious of God to give us this clear teaching about worshipping him. Left to our own devices, we would be in the dark as to how to approach him. One writer puts the problem this way: 'men are naturally incapable of knowing what forms of worship become the majesty of God, and especially what forms are suited to, and correspond with, the revelation he has made of himself at any given period.'[1]

But these elements of public worship come in the context of some broader biblical teaching on the subject. In the book of Hebrews we have one of the most significant passages addressing where we stand with respect to our public worship of God. It is worth reading this passage fully in order to draw out its major points:

> For you have not come to what may be touched, a blazing fire and darkness and gloom and a tempest and the sound of a trumpet and a voice whose words made the hearers beg that no further messages be spoken to them. For they could not endure the order that was given, 'If even a beast touches the mountain, it shall be stones.' Indeed, so terrifying was the sight that Moses said, 'I tremble with fear.' But you have come to Mount Zion and to the city of the living God, the heavenly Jerusalem, and to innumerable angels in their festal gathering, and to the assembly of the firstborn who are enrolled in heaven, and to God, the judge of all, and to

[1] Thomas E. Peck, 'The Worship of the Church,' in *Writings of Thomas E. Peck*, vol. 1 (Edinburgh: Banner of Truth Trust, 1999), p. 97.

the spirits of the righteous made perfect, and to Jesus, the mediator of a new covenant, and to the sprinkled blood that speaks a better word than the blood of Abel. See to it that you do not refuse him who is speaking (Heb. 12:18-25a).

There are at least four facets of our approach to God that Hebrews emphasizes. *First*, it is not accompanied by the visible pomp and visible danger of the approach of the Old Testament (verses 20, 21). *Second*, it is worship in which we are joining together with ongoing worship in heaven (verses 22, 23). In other words, God does not need our worship, and those who know him best worship him continually. *Third*, our worship is focused on Jesus (verse 24). He is the mediator of our covenant, and he is our high priest. We can only approach God through Jesus Christ, and any worship not focused on him is no true worship at all. *Finally*, our worship of God through Jesus Christ is fundamentally centred on what God's word has said (verse 25a). Any public worship that ignores these key elements is less than what the New Testament points us to.

But consider the benefits of this approach to God. Because we are approaching through Christ, we are coming via the priest who knows us perfectly and understands our weakness. We are coming on the basis of the sacrifice that paid for our sins fully – once and for all. We are submitting ourselves to the authority of our great king, but also to the authority of a word that is living and active. This simple, Christ-focused, Bible-centred corporate worship reflects that which we know to be true of our God, and it is used by him to fuel and sustain our growth in grace.

### *A community built by Jesus*

Jesus Christ is the focus of the church. It is his body, it is founded on his promises, its worship is centred on and guided by his word. All the growth that Christians experience in the church is growth for which the triune God – Father, Son, and Holy Spirit – deserves the credit. Baptism, commanded by Jesus and done in the name of the Trinity, is the entry point of the visible church.

Jesus Christ also promised to continue to build his church, even against the gates of death and hell itself. This is the great guarantee that he makes when his disciple Peter confesses him to be 'the Christ, the Son of the living God' (Matt. 16:16). Jesus explains that this confession lays the groundwork for the new assembly that he will build: 'And I tell you, you are Peter, and on this rock I will build my church, and the gates of hell shall not prevail against it' (Matt. 16:18).

Nothing can stop what Jesus has determined to do in his church. And the church, for all its outward failings, plays an integral role in what God is doing in the world. And it also plays a vital role in what God is doing, by his grace, in the lives of individual Christians.

# 8

# The Meal that Nourishes
## 1 Corinthians 11:26

Up to this point in our study we have examined the broad contours of what it means to grow in grace. We also have seen the ways in which the Lord Jesus Christ – our King, Saviour, and the embodiment of grace – graciously provides for us in our weakness: he is our prophet, priest, and king. There are so many ways in which this gives us comfort as we face difficulties in life. As we move forward in the Christian life we learn that growing in grace is not merely growth in an abstract understanding of principles, or simply a development of certain virtues; it involves growing in a relationship with a person.

And the Lord Jesus Christ has given us a meal at which he promises to meet with us by the Holy Spirit. This meal, which Christians refer to as communion or The Lord's Supper, plays an important role in our growth in grace, and enables us to have special fellowship with the one who is our great Saviour and friend.

## *A strange institution*

As people near the end of their lives, they often reflect with fondness on the good times they have had. Even amidst the pain, sorrow and fear that can accompany death, it is not uncommon for someone to say, 'Don't remember me like this. Remember the good times we shared.' It is those fond memories that often linger longest in the minds of those who remain after the death of a friend or a family member. Funerals often reflect this as, one by one, family members and friends remind each other of good times they shared with the one who recently departed.

But in contrast to this, as Jesus prepared to die, he gathered his disciples together and told them to remember his coming suffering and death. He did not reminisce about good times, about those moments that might have appeared to be the high points of his earthly ministry. There were no reminders of funny moments. Instead of telling his disciples *not* to remember him in his state of weakness and pain, he instituted a meal precisely to commemorate his hour of suffering.

On the surface there is something strange about this but, when we think about it more clearly, this is exactly what we should have expected. After all, Jesus repeatedly told his disciples that he had come to die for the sins of his people. From the beginning of his earthly ministry, those who understood what God was doing in Christ recognized this as well. John the Baptist cried out: 'Behold, the Lamb of God, who takes away the sin of the world!' (John 1:29b). When Jesus was still a baby, the godly priest Simeon told

Mary and Joseph, 'Behold, this child is appointed for the fall and rising of many in Israel, and for a sign that is opposed (and a sword will pierce through your own soul also), so that thoughts from many hearts are revealed' (Luke 23b, 35). Jesus was no less emphatic in spelling out his coming death as he 'set his face to go to Jerusalem' (Luke 9:51). The Gospel writers record some of these predictions for us, such as this one in Mark's Gospel:

> And they were on the road, going up to Jerusalem, and Jesus was walking ahead of them. And they were amazed, and those who followed were afraid. And taking the twelve again, he began to tell them what was going to happen to him, saying, 'See we are going up to Jerusalem, and the Son of Man will be delivered over to the chief priests and the scribes, and they will condemn him to death, and deliver him over to the Gentiles. And they will mock him and spit on him, and flog him and kill him. And after three days he will arise' (Mark 10:32-34).

Jesus could not have been clearer about his coming death and resurrection. So, in that sense, it should come as no surprise that on the eve of his crucifixion he would establish something to commemorate that event, as brutal as it was. As vital as the other events of his earthly ministry were, it was his coming death and resurrection that marked the culmination of all that he had set out to do on earth.

In light of this, at Jesus' last supper before his crucifixion, he instituted another meal to be celebrated by his followers until his return:

Now as they were eating, Jesus took bread, and after blessing it broke it and gave it to the disciples and said, 'Take, eat;
this is my body.' And he took a cup, and when he had given
thanks he gave it to them, saying, 'Drink of it, all of you, for
this is my blood of the covenant, which is poured out for
many for the forgiveness of sins. I tell you I will not drink
again of this fruit of the vine until that day when I drink
it new with you in my Father's kingdom' (Matt. 26:26-29).[1]

In instituting this simple meal of bread and wine, Jesus
commanded those who were his disciples to commemorate
his death and to look forward to that day when they will
enjoy Jesus' physical presence once again. Jesus also makes
it clear in these words of institution that his bloody death
was not a failure or a memory to be suppressed; rather, it
was the fulfilment of God's covenant promise, and it was
the means by which God would forgive the sins of many.

### Three words

As we move forward in the New Testament, we begin to
see with even greater clarity just how significant the cel-
ebration of the Lord's Supper is to the Christian life. We
see the earliest Christians 'breaking bread' together, which
likely is a reference to their practice of communion.[2] We
know that the congregations outside of the earliest church
in Jerusalem practised this as well, as evidenced in Paul's
instruction to the Corinthian church in 1 Corinthians 11.
Even when we move beyond the New Testament itself, we

[1] See also the institution as recorded in Mark 14:12-26 and Luke 22:7-39.
[2] See for instance, Acts 2:42.

see the earliest Christians practicing this communion meal as part of their gathered worship.

Here is an excerpt from an early record of Christian worship in the second century AD:

> And when the president has given thanks, and all the people have expressed their assent, those who are called by us deacons give to each of those present to partake of the bread and wine mixed with water over which the thanksgiving was pronounced, and to those who are absent they carry away a portion. And this food is called among us *Eucharist*, of which no one is allowed to partake but the man who believes that the things which we teach are true, and who has been washed with the washing that is for the remission of sins, and unto regeneration, and who is so living as Christ has enjoined.[1]

When we look at the Scriptures to understand the significance of this meal, we see the apostle Paul uses three terms to describe it. Each of these terms underscores something significant about the meal and its purpose. By understanding each, we will begin to see why the Lord's Supper is such a vital aspect of our growth in grace.

First, both Jesus and the Apostle Paul refer to the meal as a *remembrance* or a commemoration. The bread, according to Paul, is a remembrance of Jesus' body and the cup is a remembrance of Jesus' blood. This constant reminder is critical to our own growth in grace. The Lord knows how prone we are to forgetting the most important things

---

[1] Taken from Justin Martyr, *First Apology*, chapter 66.

in life and finding ourselves sidetracked to that which is peripheral. Even Jesus' own disciples, having heard him speak again of his coming death, failed to understand its significance even as it happened.[1] How much more prone can we be to do the same! Individuals, and even whole congregations, can begin to think that Christianity has something else at its centre other than Jesus' death and resurrection on behalf of sinners. We see this happen in the case of the Galatian church, which was in danger of abandoning the gospel of Christ; we see it in the Ephesian church in Revelation, which had abandoned its true love; and in the many churchgoers in the last days, who, according to Paul, would abandon sound teaching.[2] This danger can befall ministers of the gospel as well, which is why Paul was so emphatic to say, 'For I decided to know nothing among you except Jesus Christ and him crucified' (1 Cor. 2:2). We are prone to distraction, prone to forgetfulness, and prone to be led astray into that which is at best peripheral. We need a constant reminder, and the Lord's Supper provides that for us.

Second, Paul also refers to communion as a *proclamation*. He writes, 'For as often as you eat this bread and drink this cup, you proclaim the Lord's death until he comes' (1 Cor. 11:26). Partaking in the Lord's Supper in faith is a public act. When framed by the teaching of Scripture, communion is a declaration of our allegiance to Jesus Christ,

---

[1] See, for instance, the account of two disciples after Jesus' death in Luke 24:13-35.

[2] These examples are found in Gal. 5:2-4; Rev. 2:4; and 2 Tim. 5:3.

and a public announcement of the centrality of his word and his sacrifice to us as individuals and to our congregations. In times of persecution and unbelief, this public proclamation is especially significant. As we commonly say to one another, 'Actions speak louder than words.' And the action of openly declaring commitment to Jesus Christ by participating with other believers in this meal can have profound public consequences. Many Christians have been persecuted for the public acts of baptism and the Lord's Supper. For unbelievers who watch from the outside, communion shows clearly that which we hold most dear, and it is a testimony to our confidence in the promises Christ has made to forgive those who come to him in faith, and to return again in glory for our salvation.

Finally, we must consider a third word which Paul uses to describe the Lord's Supper. In 1 Corinthians 10, Paul uses the word *participation* to describe the significance of the meal. This participation (or 'communion'), is actually shared both with those whom we partake the meal alongside, and also with Jesus himself. An extended quotation along with some explanation is necessary at this point. But make no mistake, this is one of the reasons why we must consider the Lord's Supper in any discussion of our growth in grace.

Paul writes:

> The cup of blessing that we bless, is it not a participation in the blood of Christ? The bread we break, it is not a participation in the body of Christ? Because there is one bread,

we who are one body, for we all partake of the one bread
… You cannot drink the cup of the Lord and the cup of
demons. You cannot partake of the table of the Lord and
the table of demons. Shall we provoke the Lord to jealousy?
Are we stronger than he? (1 Cor. 10:16, 17, 21, 22).

This requires some explanation, so it is important to
understand the context of what Paul is writing. Paul is
writing to command the Corinthians to flee from idolatry
(1 Cor. 10:14). In that context, however, he reminds them
of the deep significance and the profound implications of
their practice of the Lord's Supper. According to Paul, when
we partake of the Lord's Supper as it is rightly ordered by
the word of God, we enjoy special communion with Jesus
Christ himself and with one another as his body. This is
why the meal is so often called *communion*. But how is
this possible? After all, Jesus Christ ascended into heaven
and he is seated there at the Father's right hand. Jesus is
not physically present when we celebrate the supper, but
he is present with us spiritually through the Holy Spirit
whom he sent. When we eat the bread, Paul says, it is a
participation in Christ's body; when we drink the cup, it
is a participation in Christ's blood. The Lord's Supper is
not simply a time for us to remember in our minds, it is a
time to share by the Holy Spirit. And the same Holy Spirit
who does this also works to bring us, who are so different
from one another, into one body.

We need all of these things to grow in grace. We need
to have a constant re-centring, a reminder of what is most

important; we grow through regular substantial proclamation; and we are fed, comforted and strengthened as we participate as one body with the Lord Jesus Christ. What a good gift from our gracious Saviour! As John Calvin, the great sixteenth-century pastor and Reformer, puts it:

> So then, let us recognize, when now the Supper is offered to us, that our Lord Jesus wishes that we might find all our goodness in him, He draws near to us through his goodness. It is true that he does not leave his heavenly glory, he need not descend here below to communicate to us his body and his blood, but although we are far away from him, yet he does not cease to feed us with his body and his blood.[1]

[1] John Calvin, *Sermons*, pp 254-5.

# PART 4

## THE LIFE OF GRACE

# 9

# Dead to Sin
# Romans 6:11

## Brought to life

Up to this point, we have seen portraits of what growth in grace looks like. Perhaps more significantly, we have reflected on the incarnation of the Lord Jesus Christ and his offices of prophet, priest, and king, which are fundamental to our life as Christians. We cannot possibly move forward as believers in Jesus Christ without knowing who he is. In addition, we cannot move forward if we do not make use of the means he has ordained for our growth. If we are not part of a gospel congregation and if we are not participating regularly in the meal he has provided, then we will be missing out on the very things Jesus has designed for us to enjoy.

All of these things are crucial for us, but they mean nothing if we are not born again spiritually. We have already seen that our salvation is all by grace alone, through faith alone.[1] But it is important now to look in more detail about the way in which God's grace worked in our lives to bring us to saving faith in Christ.

The basic image the Bible uses to talk about this transition is the image of new life. And the source of that new spiritual life is God himself – working through his word and working by his Spirit. Because the Holy Spirit and the word work together, the Bible can talk about our conversion as a work of the Holy Spirit or a work of God's word. For instance, emphasizing the role of the word of God, we read, 'Since you have been born again, not of perishable seed but of imperishable, through the living and abiding word of God …' (1 Pet. 1:23). And again, 'Of his own will he brought us forth by the word of truth …' (James 1:18a). Or again, 'So faith comes by hearing, and hearing through the word of Christ' (Rom. 10:18). But the Bible speaks with equal clarity about our new birth as a work of the Holy Spirit, as in Jesus' conversation with Nicodemus:

> Truly, truly I say to you, unless one is born of water and the Spirit, he cannot enter the kingdom of God. That which is born of flesh is flesh, and that which is born of the Spirit is spirit … The wind blows where it wishes, and you hear its sound, but you do not know where it comes from or where it is going. So it is with everyone born of the Spirit (John 3:5, 6, 8).

This pattern of God's Spirit and God's word working together is found throughout the Bible. Even in the first

---

[1] See chapter 2 above.

chapter of Genesis, when the personhood of the Holy Spirit has not yet been revealed clearly, we see God create by his *word*, with his *Spirit* 'hovering' throughout the process (Gen. 1:2). We also know that the Holy Spirit is responsible for God's written word, the Bible: 'Knowing this first of all, that no prophecy of Scripture comes from someone's own interpretation. For no prophecy was ever produced by the will of man, but men spoke from God as they were carried along by the Holy Spirit' (2 Pet. 1:20, 21). In other words, God's word and Spirit work together in creation, and God's written word is produced by the work of God's Spirit. It is no surprise, then, that Peter uses the name of the human author (the term Scripture), and the name of the Holy Spirit interchangeably: 'Brothers, the *scripture* had to be fulfilled, which the *Holy Spirit* spoke beforehand by the mouth of *David* …' (Acts 1:16, emphasis added).

There is a wonderful illustration of the intimate connection between the power of God's word and the work of God's Spirit found in Ezekiel 37. In this chapter, the prophet is taken into the wilderness and shown a pile of dry bones. He is told to prophesy – to proclaim God's word – to the dry bones. As the prophet preaches to the bones, they come together, they grow sinews and flesh and they stand in line. They are described in the end as 'an exceedingly great army' (Ezek. 37:10). What does this illustrate? The Lord explains it this way: 'And I will put my Spirit within you, and you shall live, and I will place you in your own land. Then you shall know that I am the LORD; I have spoken and I will do it, declares the LORD'

(Ezek. 37:14). Once again, the word of God is used by the Spirit of God to do the work of God.

Although most of us are conscious of our conversion as a work of God's word, the Bible is very clear that the reason God's word sank deeply into our hearts, the reason we were moved to place our trust in the Lord Jesus for our salvation, is because of the work of the Holy Spirit. God the Holy Spirit gave us new spiritual life.

### Dead to sin

Because of this new spiritual life given to us by the Holy Spirit, the Bible tells us that, in an ultimate sense, we have died to sin as Christians. This is a difficult teaching to accept since all of us struggle with sin. In fact, the Bible tells us that if any of us claim to be without sin, we are simply deceiving ourselves.[1] So in order to understand how the Bible can simultaneously remind us of our ongoing sin *and* tell us that we have died to sin, we need to dive a little more deeply into the work of the triune God – Father, Son, and Holy Spirit – in giving us new life spiritually.

We have seen that the major way the Bible talks about our conversion is to speak of it in terms of new birth or new life – brought about by the Holy Spirit working through the proclamation of the Scriptures. This new spiritual life given to us by the Holy Spirit is profound. Though we may not immediately feel a difference at the time of our conversion, a change has been made by God nonetheless. A number

[1] 1 John 1:8: 'If we say we have no sin, we deceive ourselves, and the truth is not in us.'

of theologians have summarized this change brought about by the Holy Spirit, but perhaps nowhere is it stated as concisely as by the Synod of Dort, which developed a set of canons (principles or standards) in 1618–19. Here is what these canons say about the change brought about in us by the Holy Spirit:

> But when God accomplishes his good pleasure in the elect, or works in them true conversion, he not only causes the gospel to be externally preached to them, and powerfully illuminates their minds by his Holy Spirit, that they may rightly under and discern the things of the Spirit of God; but by the efficacy of the same regenerating Spirit he pervades the inmost recesses of man; he opens the closed and softens the hardened heart, and circumcises that which was uncircumcised; infuses new qualities into the will, which, though heretofore dead, he quickens; from being evil, disobedient, and refractory, he renders it good, obedient, and pliable; actuates and strengthens it, that like a good tree, it may bring forth the fruits of good actions.[1]

This language may seem a little dense to us today, but it is worth noticing two things that are mentioned here. The first is that the Holy Spirit who regenerates us (gives us new birth spiritually) also 'pervades the inmost recesses.' In other words, the Holy Spirit works in the deepest parts of us. Along those same lines, notice a second phrase: he 'infuses new qualities into the will, which, though heretofore [up to this point] dead, he quickens [brings to life].'

---

[1] Canons of the Synod of Dort, 'Third and Fourth Head, Article 11.'

This deep theological teaching about what the Holy Spirit does in and for us is supplemented in the Scriptures by another deep theological truth: when we are saved by Christ, we are not only regenerated and indwelt by the Holy Spirit, *we are also united to Christ himself.* This is taught in many places in the New Testament, but perhaps a sampling will make the point clear.

When speaking about the good news of Jesus being proclaimed to Gentiles, Paul writes: 'To them God chose to make known how great among the Gentiles are the riches of the glory of this mystery, *which is Christ in you, the hope of glory*' (Col. 1:27, emphasis added). Later in that same letter, Paul writes this:

> … and you have been filled *in him*, who is also the head of all rule and authority. *In him* also you were circumcised with a circumcision made without hands, by putting off the body of the flesh, by the circumcision of Christ, having been buried *with him in baptism*, in which you were also raised *with him* through faith in the powerful working of God who raised him from the dead. And you, who were dead in your trespasses and the uncircumcision of your flesh, God made alive *together with him* … (Col. 2:10-13, emphasis added).

This theme is so pervasive that Paul summarizes his own Christian conversion in this way: 'I have been crucified with Christ. It is no longer I who live, but Christ who lives in me' (Gal. 2:20a). And this gets to the key issue in understanding our growth in grace. Since the Holy Spirit indwells the deepest reaches of our being, and since we are united spiritually to Jesus Christ, we are no longer slaves to sin and death.

The grip of slavery to sin and death has been replaced by the new life brought about by the Holy Spirit and through our union with Jesus Christ. In a very real sense, true Christians are dead to sin because of these deep spiritual realities.

### Die to sin

But we still sin! So what does the Bible command us to do about this as we grow in grace? First, the Scriptures tell us that we must understand these realities and consider them to be true. After summarizing the doctrine of our union with Christ, Paul puts it this way: 'So you must consider yourselves dead to sin and alive to God in Christ Jesus' (Rom. 6:11). This is a straightforward command, but when we think about all the theological heavy-lifting that we needed to do just to understand how Paul could say this, and when we combine that with the ongoing reality of our sinful state, we begin to realize how difficult this can be in practice.

As Christians, we need to reflect each day on the realities of the Holy Spirit living in us and of our union with Jesus Christ himself. Even when Christians are by themselves and feeling tempted, they are not alone but are in vital union with God. The same Holy Spirit who brought us from death to life dwells inside us. The same Christ who rose from the dead is united spiritually to us. This is meant to be a tremendous comfort and strength, but we need to reflect upon it.

The second major command that naturally follows this reality is that we cannot allow sin to reign in us as if it were in charge. Right after telling us to 'consider' these things, Paul then writes, 'Let not sin therefore reign in your mortal body, to make you obey its passions. Do not present your members to sin as instruments of unrighteousness, but present yourself to God as those who have been brought from death to life …' (Rom. 6:12, 13a). Just as we need to consider the realities of our new life, reflecting deeply upon their implications, so too we need to stop acting as if sin were our slave-master any longer.

These are difficult commands, but they are eminently practical. They require a lifetime of exertion on our part, and they are grounded on theological truths which are difficult to understand and impossible to fully grasp in this life. But this is where we must focus our attention. And in so doing, we will be entering into faithful service of our Saviour, the substance of which is the subject of our next chapter.

# 10

# Slaves to Righteousness
# Romans 6:18

## *A difficult teaching*

It is difficult to understand the way the Bible uses the word
'dead' to describe our relationship with sin. As we have
seen, this is due at least partly to our ongoing experience
of indwelling sin. We still sin in many ways so we have a
difficult time wrapping our minds around the Bible's teaching that we have died to sin. But there is another important
doctrine that goes along with this one and it is similarly
both difficult and crucial to our understanding of what
it means to grow in grace. Just after the Bible reminds us
that we are dead to sin, it then tells us that we are *enslaved*
to righteousness.

Because of the recent history of slavery, particularly in
North America, the language of enslavement carries with
it many troubling connotations. To be enslaved is to miss
out on freedom. It means having no meaningful input in

your life or work. Often slaves were and are abused and, whatever their conditions, the one constant feature of slavery is that involves being owned by another person. Since these facts about slavery are so firmly fixed in our minds, many consider it a Christian duty to oppose slavery at any time under any conditions.

But when we turn to the pages of the New Testament, we see that Christians refer to themselves directly (or are referred to by the author) over forty times as slaves! Most of the time they are called 'slaves of God' or 'slaves of Christ.' Sometimes, they are just referred to as 'fellow slaves.'

To take just one example: the apostle Paul begins his letters by identifying himself. This was the standard way of writing a letter in his day – by identifying the author and his credentials first. When Paul identifies himself and his credentials, though, he often uses the word 'slave.' For instance, in Romans 1:1 he starts his letter this way: 'Paul, a [*slave*] of Christ Jesus… '[1] At the beginning of Philippians he extends this title beyond himself, beginning his letter in this way: 'Paul and Timothy, [*slaves*] of Christ Jesus' (Phil. 1:1, brackets and emphasis added). And he extends it even further in two other places, reminding Christians who are in physical slavery that their more significant slavery is to Christ, and also reminding Christians who were not physical slaves of this truth: 'Likewise, he who was free

[1] Brackets and emphasis added. The ESV, along with some other modern English translations, renders this word as 'servant' to avoid the negative connotations associated with modern slavery. In the ESV, the more accurate translation, 'slave,' is indicated in the margin.

when called is a [*slave*] of Christ' (1 Cor. 7:22b, brackets
and emphasis added).[1] Paul was not alone in designating
himself and other Christian believers in this way. Luke,
James, Peter, Jude, Mary and Simeon each do the same.

And make no mistake, many of the ideas that we identify
with slavery in modern times were no less true of slavery
in the ancient world. Although many slaves in the era of
the New Testament were given great responsibility and
were sometimes even the beneficiaries of the privileges of
education and esteem, one simple fact remained. As one
scholar puts it: 'A Roman could buy, rent or sell a slave, as
he would a piece of property. An owner's right to use and
dispose of his slave as he wished was called *dominium*, "the
right of absolute ownership."'[2] In other words, whatever the
differences between our conception of slavery and what
took place in Paul's day the fact remains that, then and
now, to be enslaved was to be owned by another. The fact
that the apostle would use the language of slavery to talk
about himself, his fellow ministers and every Christian can
be troubling to us. How does this talk of slavery fit with
the emphasis in Scripture of our being set free from sin,
death and the law?

### Free to be enslaved

The key to understanding this difficult doctrine of our
enslavement as Christians is first to understand what the

[1] For the passages referring to physical slaves being slaves of Christ,
see Eph. 6:6.
[2] Murray J. Harris, *Slave of Christ: A New Testament Metaphor for Total
Devotion to Christ* (Downers Grove, IL: Intervaristy, 1999) p. 37.

Bible says about our freedom and its scope. Jesus directly addresses the issue of slavery and freedom when speaking with some Jewish people who had begun to follow him. He begins by speaking of the freedom that the truth of his word would bring: 'If you abide in my word, you are truly my disciples, and you will know the truth, and the truth will set you free' (John 5:31). After Jesus speaks about freedom his hearers, as is so often the case, misunderstand what he is saying. They think that his words are inappropriate. But Jesus is speaking of something deeper than bondage to other human beings. He responds to their questions by saying, 'Truly, truly, I say to you, everyone who practises sin is a slave to sin' (John 8:34). This is the lasting and eternal bondage from which Jesus came to redeem his people.

The apostle Paul builds on these words of Jesus when writing about our freedom in Christ. In Romans 6 he writes, 'Do you not know that if you present yourselves to anyone as obedient slaves, you are slaves to the one whom you obey, either to sin which leads to death, or of obedience which leads to righteousness?' (Rom. 6:16). In the Bible, the question is not whether we will be enslaved to something, it is rather to whom or to what will we be enslaved?

As Paul explains the various aspects of our freedom, he connects this freedom with slavery to Jesus Christ. He writes that we are not enslaved to sin, which means we are not under law, we are not being led to death, we are not slaves to impurity and ever-increasing wickedness, we are not enslaved to things that make us ashamed. But we are now enslaved to righteousness, under the rule of grace, which leads to righteousness, obedience to sound teaching, the offering our bodies in holy service, being enslaved to God.[1] To be free from sin is to be enslaved to righteousness. And the outcome of this is eternal life.

### Christ our master

Our liberation from sin does not simply free us to be our own masters. That would mean following our own sinful desires and being led into greater bondage. Rather, the Scriptures tell us that to be freed from sin and to be enslaved to righteousness means that we serve a new and far better master, Jesus, whom Christians have always declared to be their Lord. The apostle Paul again states this concisely, 'For what we proclaim is not ourselves, but Jesus Christ as Lord, with ourselves as your [*slaves*] for Jesus' sake' (2 Cor. 4:5, brackets and emphasis added). To call Jesus 'Lord' is not simply to acknowledge his deity (although in many places in the Bible it means just that), but rather to admit your own slavery to him.

If Christ is our master, then we must obey him. Whatever else our freedom in Christ means, it cannot mean that we are free to make our own rules or choose our own priorities. Sadly, some leaders within the church teach this kind of thing. They use the language of freedom in Christ as a cover for treating sin lightly. This false teaching is widespread, but it is not new. Paul encountered it very early on in his ministry, which is why he wrote these words: 'For you were called to freedom, brothers. Only do not use

---

[1] See Rom. 6:15-23 for these comparisons and contrasts.

your freedom as an opportunity for the flesh, but through love serve one another' (Gal. 5:13). The apostle Peter had to remind Christians of much the same thing. He wrote: 'Live as people who are free, not using your freedom as a cover-up for evil, but living as [*slaves*] of God' (1 Pet. 2:16, brackets and emphasis added). This redefinition of Christian freedom must have been prevalent since Peter's portrait of the false teachers in his day incorporates this description: 'They promise them [their hearers] freedom, but they themselves are slaves of corruption. For whatever overcomes a person, to that he is enslaved' (2 Pet. 2:19, brackets added).

The idea that Christian freedom implies an absence of boundaries or a removal of all restraints is a tired old heresy that has been with us from the beginning but, as we have seen, it is counter to the most basic logic of the master-slave relationship. Jesus owns us. He has purchased our freedom with his own blood. We owe to him our complete allegiance as our Lord.

This means, first of all, that our abiding objective should be growing in Christlikeness. Since we are slaves of Jesus Christ, he tells us that we are to strive to be like him, especially in the midst of persecution. Jesus says, 'A disciple is not above his teacher, nor a [*slave*] above his master. It is enough for the disciple to be like his teacher and the [*slave*] like his master. If they have called the master of the house Beelzebul, how much more will they malign those of his household' (Matt. 10:24, 25, brackets and emphasis added). Our service to Christ means that we cannot shy away from identifying with him and our goal should be conformity to him. It should not surprise us that this slavery to Christ involves suffering. Jesus drew our attention to this when highlighting our role as his slaves.

As we strive to live in conformity to Jesus' character and example, we also need to strive to represent him well. One example of this comes in Paul's letter to Timothy. Timothy was faced with a difficult ministry. There were false teachers in his congregation, and others who simply liked an argument. But Timothy was called to a higher standard. He could not take part in this kind of foolishness. Why? Because he was a slave of Christ: 'And the Lord's [*slave*] must not be quarrelsome, but kind to everyone, able to teach, patiently enduring evil, correcting his opponents with gentleness …' (2 Tim. 2:24, 25b, brackets and emphasis added). To be a slave of Jesus Christ means not only identifying with him and imitating him, it also means acting in a way that is becoming to our service of him. Jesus has rules for the behaviour and comportment of his slaves. This extends to the use of our bodies in every respect. As Paul reminds all of us, 'You are not your own, for you were bought with a price. So glorify God in your body' (1 Cor. 6:19b, 20).

### Christ our friend

The Bible provides a liberating message for those enslaved to sin. There is freedom offered in Jesus Christ. He sets sinners free from their bondage, making them slaves of God, leading to holiness, righteousness, and life. This is indeed good news! But Jesus gives us even more good news as he discusses our service to him. Even those who have been liberated from terrible bondage in order to serve a perfect master in a good and healthy cause would not expect to be friends with the master whom they serve. They would never imagine that the master would explain to them his commands or his purposes. But our master, the Lord Jesus Christ, has done just this. Jesus reframes our slavery and obedience to him:

> You are my friends if you do what I command you. No longer do I call you [*slaves*], for the [*slave*] does not know what his master is doing; but I have called you friends, for all that I have heard from my Father I have made known to you. You did not choose me, but I chose you and appointed you that you should go and bear much fruit and that your fruit should abide, so that whatever you ask the Father in my name, he may give it to you. These things I command you, so that you will love one another (John 15:15-17, brackets and emphasis added).

We cannot shy away from speaking of Jesus as our Lord and ourselves as his slaves. This is the teaching of Scripture and it is placed against the backdrop of the freedom that we have as Christians from sin and death. This slavery involves obligations of course, but it also involves unimaginable privileges. Not only does it lead to holiness now and eternal life in the future but it also involves the intimacy of friendship with Jesus, who won our freedom and commands our loving obedience.

## 11

# It's Not About You
# Mark 10:43

### *In the beginning*

There is a glorious paradox in the Bible's teaching regarding our slavery to Jesus Christ. On the one hand, since we are slaves, we owe total allegiance to another person. On the other hand, since Jesus Christ also calls us friends, we realize that this total allegiance comes with privileges of access that we can hardly imagine – privileges that would be unheard of in the normal relationship between a master and a slave. More than that, our slavery to God is set against the backdrop of the radical liberation we have been given. Redeemed by Christ's blood, we are set free from bondage to sin.

But we must not forget that, while God has lavished rich blessings on us in Jesus Christ and given us a life of meaning, purpose, and acceptance in him, our lives are not our own. The course of history is not just about our forgiveness and eternal happiness. In an ultimate sense, everything in the universe is about bringing glory to the triune God.

We see this truth clearly when we pick up our Bibles and begin reading on page one. The book of Genesis begins with God: 'In the beginning, God created the heavens and the earth' (Gen. 1:1). By the end of the chapter, we are introduced to humankind, specifically to Adam and Eve. What sets them apart from all the other creatures is the fact that they, and they alone, are created in the image of God. From the start there is a God-ward focus for everything in creation. He is the Creator and his highest creatures are given such prominence precisely because of their resemblance to him.

So it will not surprise us to see that at the end of the Bible the focus is still on the triune God. In the book of Revelation John sees a vision of the eternal city – the new heavens and the new earth. At the eternal culmination of human history God is the focus:

> And I saw no temple in the city, for its temple is the Lord God the Almighty and the Lamb. And the city has no need of sun or moon to shine on it, for the glory of God gives it light, and its lamp is the Lamb. By its light will the nations walk, and the kings of the earth will bring their glory into it, and its gates will never be shut by day – and there will be no night there. They will bring into it the glory and honour of the nations. But nothing unclean will ever enter it, nor anyone who does what is detestable or false, but only those whose names are written in the Lamb's book of life. Then

the angel showed me the river of the water of life, bright as crystal, flowing from the throne of God and of the Lamb (Rev. 21:22–22:1).

Notice that everything in this vision is centred on God: his visible presence removes the need for a temple; his glory provides the light, acting as a beacon for all who enter; he alone receives tribute from all nations; his book determines those who are present; and the river of life flows from his throne. It is a God-centred picture of eternity. It is the perfect place for redeemed humanity precisely because everything is focused on the Lord.

This vision of the future and these realities of creation should give shape and focus to our lives as Christians. Human beings are naturally self-centred. We are prone to see ourselves as the centre of the universe, as the stars of the show. When our minds wander, we naturally think of plans for ourselves, how our lives can fulfil our wishes. Even when we stop to think of others, it is most often in relationship to ourselves. Our society tends to reinforce this impulse. We are told that we will be most healthy and fulfilled if we think first about our own satisfaction.

But the Bible gives us an entirely different picture of ultimate human satisfaction. We are created by God and our lasting satisfaction will only come through our enjoyment of him. The Westminster Shorter Catechism states this in a pithy way. Its first question asks: 'What is the chief end of man?' The answer is this: 'Man's chief end is to glorify God and to enjoy him forever.' This makes sense of all that we have seen in the Scriptures and it provides purpose to our lives. To grow in grace is to have our lives shaped more and more by this overriding objective: we exist to glorify and enjoy God.

The apostle Paul understood this. He recognized that even the mundane activities and decisions of life need to be done to God's glory. He writes, 'So, whether you eat or drink, or whatever you do, do all to the glory of God' (1 Cor. 10:31). This is what growing in grace looks like. The focus of our lives needs to move away from our own ambitions and desires and instead be centred on bringing glory to the God who created us and who will receive our tribute for all eternity.

### *Greatness redefined*

This shift in focus – away from ourselves and to the Lord – will have profound ramifications. What the Bible teaches is that orienting our lives around God and his glory inevitably causes us to change our priorities and redefine success.

Jesus' disciples had trouble understanding this, just as we do today. One of the most vivid examples of their misunderstanding is shown to us in the Gospel of Mark. The background of the story is one of Jesus' clearest declarations of his impending execution on a cross. Jesus is recorded as saying,

> See, we are going to Jerusalem, and the Son of Man will be delivered over to the chief priests and the scribes, and they will condemn him to death and deliver him over to the Gentiles. And they will mock him and spit on him,

and flog him and kill him. And after three days he will rise (Mark 10:33, 34).

It is hard to imagine a clearer outline of the events to come than that. It is a concise statement of exactly what would take place when Jesus and his disciples entered Jerusalem. Yet surprisingly, Jesus' disciples do not pick up on this. They still seem blinded by their own expectations of what kind of a Messiah Jesus would be and what kind of mission they were on.

We know they were confused because the next thing that is recorded is a request by James and John. But it is not just any request. They ask Jesus to do whatever they want. When Jesus probes for more detail, it turns out that what they wanted was to sit on his right and his left in glory.

The Saviour graciously turns their attention from their own desires to what it is that they are really asking. He effectively reminds them again of his coming death, asking them if they are willing and able to endure what he is about to experience. They respond in the affirmative. By this point in the story, the other disciples have heard what James and John were asking. They are indignant: after all, they too wanted places of honour and glory next to Jesus. So Jesus then moves on to talk about the nature of true greatness.[1] It is worth reading Jesus' exact words at this point:

> You know that those who are considered rulers of the Gentiles lord it over them, and their great ones exercise authority over them. But it shall not be so among you.

[1] This is a summary of Mark 10:35-41.

> But whoever wants to be great among you must be your
> servant, and whoever would be first among you must be
> slave of all (Mark 10:42b-44).

Notice how Jesus begins. He acknowledges that the
way authority and greatness usually work among people
is relatively straightforward. If you are considered great, it
is because you can command others to do what you would
like done. The greater you are, the more people listen to you
and do what you have asked. One cannot help but think of
the question James and John asked Jesus at the beginning
of this encounter. Not only did they want to be honoured
above the other disciples, they also wanted Jesus to grant
them 'whatever they asked.'

But after acknowledging this general human impulse,
Jesus turns it around. 'But it shall not be so among you.'
He defines greatness, not in terms of getting others to do
what you want, but rather in terms of helping others in
humble service. He even uses the term *slavery* to describe
this, only this time the slavery is not directed to God, but
rather to other people. True greatness, according to Jesus
Christ, consists in putting our desires and needs behind
those of others among whom we live. It consists in giving,
not receiving; in slavery, not in lording our desires over
those of other people.

This vision was as radical in Jesus' day as it is in our own.
In fact, some historians have suggested that the exact word
for servant which Jesus uses – the Greek word *diakonos*
– was never before employed in such a positive sense. In

other words, no one would ever elevate someone who was in this kind of menial position. It is a word that refers to table-service, and was generally employed to describe the most menial workers in a household. Even many slaves did not do this kind of *diaconal* work. And yet our Lord indicates that the *diakonos* is the truly great one.

Of course, Jesus grounds all of this in his own death as a ransom. After declaring that his followers needed to be servants and slaves of others, he says, 'For even the Son of Man came not to be served but to serve, and to give his life as a ransom for many' (Mark 10:45). The radical redefinition of greatness is something that the Lord Jesus Christ exemplified. But he not only was the perfect example of it, his death also enables his followers to serve others in a sacrificial way.

The reason why people define greatness and hold onto authority as they do is because they view themselves as the centre of the universe and life as a zero-sum game. In other words, we can think that if someone else gains over me, I lose. And if my gaining and losing is the most important thing in life, then how can I really pour my life out in service to others? The risk is too great. But if instead we recognize that Jesus has freed and secured us by his death on the cross, then we can freely give. We have identity, peace, and hope that liberates us to live for others. We not only have the example of Jesus Christ and his service, we have the provision that his sacrifice purchased for us.

### *God's glory and our neighbour's good*

When we realize that the purpose of our lives is the glory of God and we also see that in Jesus' kingdom service to others is the very definition of greatness, this takes the focus off ourselves. This is only possible because of what the triune God has done and is doing in us by his grace. This combination of looking out for the interests of others and bringing ultimate glory to God is a central aspect of what growing in grace means for us. We are commanded to exemplify this as we function as congregations of believers – together modelling service to one another because of the forgiveness and security we have in Jesus Christ. There is no better summary of all this than Paul's words in Philippians 2. He writes this to Christian believers seeking to grow in grace:

> So if there is any encouragement in Christ, any comfort from love, any participation in the Spirit, any affection and sympathy, complete my joy by being of the same mind, having the same love, being in full accord and of one mind. Do nothing from rivalry or conceit, but in humility count others more significant than yourselves. Let each of you look not only to his own interests, but also to the interests of others. Have this mind among yourselves which is yours in Christ Jesus, who, though he was in the form of God, did not count equality with God a thing to be grasped, but emptied himself, by taking on the form of a servant, being born in the likeness of men. And being found in human form, he humbled himself by becoming obedient to the point of death, even death on a cross. Therefore God has

highly exalted him and bestowed on him the name that is above every name, so that at the name of Jesus every knee should bow, in heaven and on earth and under the earth, and every tongue confess that Jesus Christ is Lord, to the glory of God the Father (Phil. 2:1-11).

## 12

# Suffering Matters
## James 1:2

### *The formula for growth*

Because our growth in grace is ultimately a work of God in us, there are no easy step-by-step formulas. In fact, the Bible uses metaphors from agriculture (plants, fields, flowers, crops) or from human development (infants, mature men) to describe the work of sanctification, rather than using formulaic terms from self-help manuals and get-rich-quick schemes. Spiritual growth cannot be reduced to a mechanical process. We must be very suspicious of so-called Christian books that promise growth in three steps or forty days. This is just not the biblical picture. Just like the growth of a plant or a flower, our growth as Christians requires certain conditions for health and progress, but the exact form and shape will often be determined by circumstances, conditions and our starting-point.

But there are certain circumstances which, when met with faith, will certainly produce growth. The Bible is unequivocal about this. The closest the Bible comes to giving a formula for growth is when it discusses Christian suffering. When Christians experience trials, persecution, and tribulation and meet those hardships with faith, they grow. In fact, this principle is so ironclad in the Scriptures that we are even told that our times of greatest spiritual power and growth are not when we are apparently strong, but when we are weak and seem to be defeated.

Why is suffering such a vital and important part of the Christian life? There are several answers to this question.

The first is that suffering produces Christian maturity. The earliest Christians realized this. Our oldest New Testament letter was penned by James, the half-brother of Jesus Christ and a leader in the church of Jerusalem. He wrote his early epistle to Christians who were suffering great persecution for their Christian faith. Likely these Christians had been driven from their homes in Jerusalem because of the threats against their life. We might expect James to offer his condolences or to offer some facile words of comfort. What he does instead is to give them a command in the midst of their suffering: 'Count it all joy, my brothers, when you meet trials of various kinds' (James 1:2a). This almost sounds callous in our ears. It is one thing to command Christians to persevere or to stand firm in the midst of trials. But James goes further than this. He instructs his suffering Christian readers not to simply make it through trials, but to look at them with joy.

There is a good reason for James' instruction on this point, as surprising as it may be. He goes on to write this:

'For you know that the testing of your faith produces stead-fastness. And let steadfastness have its full effect, that you may be perfect and complete, lacking in nothing' (James 1:2b-4). The reason James can command Christians to look with joy on their suffering is because of what suffering leads to when met with faith. It leads first to steadfastness, then to overall maturity and growth.

This is the same logic that the apostle Paul uses when describing his own attitude toward suffering. In his letter to the Romans, he writes: 'More than that, we rejoice in our sufferings, knowing that suffering produces endurance, and endurance produces character, and character produces hope, and hope does not put us to shame, because God's love has been poured into our hearts through the Holy Spirit who has been given to us' (Rom. 5:3-5). Paul rejoices in suffering not because it is enjoyable or pleasant, but because it leads him to greater growth and maturity – to a hope that will not disappoint.

This is the consistent pattern in the Christian life. Growth in grace happens most rapidly in times of suffering. Our faith becomes deeper and our hope becomes more precious and real to us. It is no accident that, in the history of the Christian church, the greatest hymns about heaven were written in times of suffering. In the English-speaking world, our most hope-filled expressions of praise were penned by American slaves living in harsh conditions. It is in conditions of suffering that hope is strengthened. Facing trials leads us away from shallow and superficial faith and into greater and deeper Christian maturity.

Trials not only lead us to maturity, they also give us a public opportunity to show the genuineness of our faith. It is one thing for someone to claim to be a Christian, but their response to suffering will show what they are really trusting in. Just as the purity of a metal can be determined by its contact with a hot flame, so the purity of our faith can be shown when subject to the fire of suffering. Peter explains this reality when writing to some of his Christians friends scattered throughout Asia:

> In this you rejoice, though now for a little while, if necessary, you have also been grieved by various trials, so that the tested genuineness of your faith – more precious than gold that perishes though tested by fire – may be found to result in praise and glory and honour at the revelation of Jesus Christ (1 Pet. 1:7, 8).

### *The formula for power*

Even if we are convinced that suffering can lead to our growth in grace, we may still question whether or not we can minister to others effectively in the midst of suffering. Usually when trials come, we turn inward and begin to think that we need to look-out for ourselves. We tell ourselves that we need to be healthy and secure before we can begin to engage in ministry to others.

But surprisingly, the most extended and powerful meditation on the role of suffering in the life of a Christian is found in Paul's letter of 2 Corinthians. In it, Paul reflects on the role that suffering played in his life as a minister. Was it a help or a hindrance? Did it detract from his ministry or add to it?

It is clear when we read the letter that the Corinthian church to which Paul was writing believed that Paul's suffering was a sign of his weakness and failure as a minister. His life and ministry did not appear to be much of a success. Paul took this painful criticism and turned it around. He explained that his suffering should not count against his ministry. More than that, Paul considered his suffering to actually display the power of God. A sampling of quotes from the letter will show just how radical Paul's understanding of suffering actually was:

> We are afflicted in every way, but not crushed; perplexed, but not driven to despair; persecuted, but not forsaken; struck down, but not destroyed; always carrying in the body the death of Jesus, so that the life of Jesus may be manifested in our bodies. For we who live are always being given over to death for Jesus' sake, so that the life of Jesus also may be manifested in our mortal flesh. So death is at work in us, but life in you (2 Cor. 4:7-12).

Later in the same chapter, Paul shares the key to his perspective. He was looking at the unseen ways in which God was at work through his suffering:

> For this light momentary affliction is preparing for us an eternal weight of glory beyond all comparison, as we look not to the things that are seen, but to the things that are unseen. For the things that are seen are transient, but the things that are unseen are eternal (2 Cor. 4:17, 18).

For Paul, the unseen work that was happening through his suffering was of far more importance than the obvious evidence of his weakness.

Paul's radically different perspective on life causes him not only to rejoice in his suffering, but genuinely to boast in it. In one of the most remarkable sections of any of Paul's writings, he details all the suffering he has undergone, citing it as a sign of strength not weakness. 'If I must boast,' Paul writes, 'I will boast of the things that show my weakness' (2 Cor. 11:30). He goes on to describe a very specific form of weakness. He admits to asking the Lord on three occasions to remove a painful difficulty from his life. And his realization after the Lord denies this request shows clearly how Paul viewed power in the context of ministry:

> Three times I pleaded with the Lord about this, that it should leave me. But he said to me, 'My grace is sufficient for you, for *my power is made perfect in weakness.*' Therefore, I will boast all the more gladly of my weaknesses, *so that the power of Christ may rest upon me.* For the sake of Christ, I am content with weaknesses, insults, hardships, persecutions, and calamities. *For when I am weak, then I am strong* (2 Cor. 12:8-10, emphasis added).

This runs exactly counter to what the world preaches about suffering and power. Suffering and weakness are signs of a lack of spiritual vitality. We naturally gravitate toward ministry success stories, and effectiveness in ministry is often viewed as synonymous with outward growth and obvious expressions of power and glory. But for the apostle Paul, the strength of God was made perfect in weakness. To use the terminology that has been the subject of our study, we could say that growth in grace and growth in our ability to minister is forged in the context of suffering and weakness.

## *Our suffering Saviour*

As jarring as the apostle's words might be, they should not come as a complete surprise. When we look at the Gospels, we see the same pattern in the earthly ministry of the Lord Jesus Christ. The great victory at the cross appeared to be a massive defeat. In Luke 24, we can see how Jesus' death appeared even to some of his closest followers. After his resurrection, Jesus appeared to two of his followers on the road to Emmaus. They did not recognize him in his new state, and he began to speak with them about what had happened. After describing the ministry and crucifixion of Jesus, they said, 'But we had hoped that he was the one to redeem Israel. Yes, and besides all this, it is now the third day since these things happened' (Luke 24:21). These two followers saw the death of Jesus as a sign of defeat. They thought he might redeem Israel, but they now see this as an impossibility. His suffering and death undermined his claim to be the Messiah.

But of course, from our vantage point, we can see what they missed. The death of Jesus was not a great defeat, it was not a sign that Jesus had lost. In fact, combined with the resurrection, it was the turning point of all of human history. And the proclamation of the cross is the major task of Christian preachers right to this day. Paul explains it this way:

> For Jews demand signs and Greeks seek wisdom, but we preach Christ crucified, a stumbling block to Jews and folly to the Gentiles, but to those who are called, both Jews and Greeks, Christ the power of God and the wisdom of God. For the foolishness of God is wiser than men, and the weakness of God is stronger than men (1 Cor. 1:22-25).

As Christians, we know that the provision for our salvation was made by Jesus Christ on the cross. His suffering and death gave us life. It displayed the power of God, though in a way the world did not recognize. And as followers of Jesus Christ, we are called to suffer as well. It is the way in which we grow; it provides clear evidence of the reality of our faith; and it is the mark of unseen spiritual strength.

Paul considered suffering inextricably linked with our belief in Christ. He writes to the Philippian church, 'For it has been granted to you that for the sake of Christ you should not only believe in him, but also that you should suffer for his sake' (Phil. 1:29). And the apostle Peter similarly tells us not to be surprised by suffering, but rather to use it to rejoice at our closeness to Jesus as we look forward in hope:

> Beloved, do not be surprised by the fiery trial when it comes upon you to test you, as though something strange were happening to you. But rejoice insofar as you share Christ's

sufferings, that you may also rejoice and be glad when his glory is also revealed (1 Pet. 4:12, 13).

# 13

# We Shall Be Like Him
## 1 John 3:2

### *From suffering to hope*

The Christian life, like any human life in a fallen world, is a life that is filled with suffering. As Christians though, we know that suffering ultimately leads to our growth in grace. It is to be expected. And, perhaps most significantly, it is something that the Lord understands fully, since he endured rejection, suffering and death himself.

One of the ways in which suffering causes us to grow in grace is that it places hope front and centre in our lives. If things are going well, we have a tendency to forget about the hope that is ours in Christ. We neglect any thoughts about the future and about the confidence we can have because of the promises Christ has made to us. But we can hardly neglect hope when times are tough. When we are suffering, our thoughts rightly turn to the future and to the wonderful things God has promised to his children in his word. In fact, growing in grace involves growing in the knowledge of what God has promised us for the future. These promises give us confidence and hope – a kind of fuel as we labour in our lives right now.

## *Home at last*

Although Jesus' disciples did not seem to understand much about his impending death and resurrection, they did seem to understand that he was leaving them, at least at the very end. In John's Gospel we are given an account of the last meal that Jesus ate with his disciples before his crucifixion and there it seems to have finally set in: Jesus was going away. Of course, it comes as no surprise that the disciples misunderstood the nature of his departure. At one point, they seem to be asking him for directions in order to follow! But the fact that he was leaving seems to have sunk in.

In the midst of the discussion about Jesus' departure, Jesus makes a startling promise. After urging them to continue trusting in God, he said:

> In my Father's house are many rooms. If it were not so, would I have told you that I go to prepare a place for you? And if I go and prepare a place for you, I will come again and will take you to myself, that where I am you may be also (John 14:2, 3).

The first thing that should strike us when we read this promise is the remarkable kindness of Jesus. He was about to be executed on a cross. Apart from the physical agony that he would endure, there was also the weight of bearing the deserved punishment of all who would believe in him. We see something of his pain when he prays shortly after this in the Garden of Gethsemane. Yet even though he knows this is just a few short hours away, he still focusses on the encouragement of his followers. And his encouragement has three parts to it.

The first aspect of Jesus' statement explains the nature of the Father's house. It is a place of many rooms, according to Jesus. The word that is translated 'rooms' in this case can refer to dwelling places or even a home. In other words, Jesus is saying that in God's house there is room for many people. All who come to God in faith will find a true and eternal home.

Depending on our background, we can underestimate the significance of this statement. Many of us have grown up taking a home for granted. We have not known what it is to be without a dwelling place, somewhere safe that we can call our own. But many know exactly what it is to have no home. In fact, Jesus described his own life in this way, saying, 'Foxes have holes, and birds of the air have nests, but the Son of Man has nowhere to lay his head' (Luke 9:58). Whether or not we can identify with this material condition, most of us know something about feeling displaced. We even use phrases such as 'I'm not quite at home in this place.' What we mean is that something does not feel quite right. But Jesus assures his followers that God's house has a dwelling place for each of us. There is a room in the Father's house for all who follow Jesus.

Not only that, but Jesus told his disciples that, after his leaving, he would prepare a specific place for them. The rooms in the house of our heavenly Father are not simply sterile and uniform. They are prepared by Jesus for us. We all know the difference between looking at the dimensions of a room as it is being constructed and seeing a room after it has been painted, furnished and decorated. The first glimpse might assure us that there will be enough space in the room for its purpose; the second will confirm its true suitability. When we see a room furnished and decorated, we now know it is just right for living in. Jesus promises not just enough space, but a specially prepared space in which we can perfectly dwell, knowing that we are at home.

Notice that Jesus does not end there. He promises lastly that he will come back and take his followers to be with him. The dwelling which Jesus describes is one in which his followers will receive a special welcome. Jesus will bring them there himself. And perhaps more amazing than that, when he brings them, it will be so that they can dwell with him. As Christians, we will never be truly at home until we are at home with Jesus Christ. As the apostle Paul reminded the Philippian church,

> But our citizenship is in heaven, and from it we await a Saviour, the Lord Jesus Christ, who will transform our lowly body to be like his glorious body, by the power that enables him even to subject all things to himself (Phil. 3:20, 21).

### *The transformation of our bodies*

Perhaps you did not catch the second part of that quotation from Philippians. If not, re-read it. You will notice that Paul reminds Christians of their heavenly citizenship and points them toward the coming of Jesus Christ. But then, rather than focusing on the welcome into God's heavenly house that we will receive, Paul instead looks forward to something else – the transformation of our bodies. This idea that we will have transformed bodies for eternity is something bound up in the Scriptures of both the Old Testament and the New Testament. It is a foundational tenet of Christian belief, and it is a conviction on which all who are growing in grace must rest their hope.

The idea that believers would live in transformed bodies is found in the Old Testament in several places, although it is more clearly taught in the New Testament. In the book of Job, for instance, we see a believer suffering greatly. In the midst of his suffering, Job expresses his certainty about the future, in words which underscore his belief in a bodily resurrection: 'And after my skin has thus been destroyed, yet in my flesh I shall see God, whom I shall see for myself, and my eyes shall behold, and not another' (Job 19:26, 27). Job's statement is remarkable because he acknowledges that his (current) skin will decay and be destroyed, yet, after that, he will be in the flesh to see God, beholding him with his own eyes.

Later, in the book of Daniel, the prophet is given a vision of the future. The culmination of this future prophecy involves the bodily resurrection. We read, 'And many of those who sleep in the dust of the earth shall awake, some to everlasting life, some to shame and everlasting contempt' (Dan. 12:2). For the ancient Jewish people reading their Bibles, this was another clear promise of bodily resurrection. In fact, this led them to embrace burial practices that preserved the remains of the dead. They expected a bodily resurrection at the end, and looked forward to it with hope in the midst of their suffering.

Jesus seems to build upon this expectation. In John's Gospel, he says,

> An hour is coming when all who are in the tombs will hear his [Jesus'] voice and come out, those who have done good to the resurrection of life, and those who have done evil to the resurrection of judgment (John 5:29).

In Jesus' teaching the bodily resurrection was a sure and certain hope. He often used this expectation to teach about his own bodily resurrection, and he also talked about the spiritual resurrection of those who trusted and followed him. But his teaching on the future bodily resurrection was consistent with that of the Old Testament.

The apostles also consistently taught about this future bodily resurrection. Their confidence and understanding of this event was bolstered by the fact that Jesus had been raised from the dead already. Paul writes,

> But in fact Christ has been raised from the dead, the firstfruits of those who have fallen asleep. For as by a man came death, by a man has come also the resurrection of the dead (1 Cor. 15:20, 21).

The resurrection of Jesus Christ was the guarantee of the future resurrection of believers and, by looking at the resurrection of Jesus, we can begin to understand something of our future resurrection. Paul writes about the order of these things in this way: 'But each in his own order: Christ the firstfruits, then at his coming those who belong to Christ' (1 Cor. 15:22).

This hope ought to change the way we look at our lives today. In the first place, it reminds us that our bodily struggles are only temporary. All of us eventually begin to feel the effects of aging on our bodies; many of us struggle because of weakness or sickness; every one of us has seen the effects of disease ravage the body and mind of someone who was formerly strong and healthy. No matter what physical failings we have, we can look forward to new bodies one day. As Paul puts it: 'It is sown in dishonour; it is raised in glory. It is sown in weakness; it is raised in power' (1 Cor. 15:43).

Not only will our physical bodies experience a transformation from weakness to strength, they will also be transformed from decaying mortal bodies to eternal heavenly ones. No matter how strong we may appear, the fact remains that, unless the Lord returns in our lifetime, we will one day die. Our physical bodies will decay. But the truth about the bodily resurrection reminds us that there will be a time when death will finally be defeated. Paul writes of this in his great chapter on the bodily resurrection:

Behold! I tell you a mystery. We shall not all sleep, but we shall all be changed, in a moment, in the twinkling of an eye, at the last trumpet. For the trumpet will sound, and the dead will be raised imperishable, and we shall be changed. For this perishable body must put on the imperishable, and this mortal body must put on immortality. When the perishable puts on the imperishable, and the mortal puts on immortality, then shall come to pass the saying that is written: 'Death is swallowed up in victory.' O death, where is your victory? O death, where is your sting? (1 Cor. 15:51-55).

This final victory over death, won by the Lord Jesus Christ, will be demonstrated clearly in our new, eternal bodies. The Bible speaks about this as our 'glorification.'[1] Another way of saying this is to say that we will finally be made like our resurrected Saviour. In the midst of our struggles here and now, we are told that focusing on this reality is a vital part of our growth in grace. The apostle John makes this connection, writing, 'Beloved, we are God's children now, and what we will be has not yet appeared; but we know that when he appears we shall be like him, because we shall see him as he is. And everyone who thus hopes in him purifies himself as he is pure' (1 John 3:2, 3).

As we conclude our study on growth in grace, we need to spend time reflecting with wonder on the future glorification of our bodies, along with our reflection on the place Jesus Christ has prepared for us for eternity. This kind of

[1] In Rom. 8:38, Paul writes, 'And those whom he justified, he also glorified.'

focus on the future is essential as we face the challenges of life and the inevitable challenges to our Christian growth. It not only provides encouragement about what one day will be, it also reminds us of who is at work within us, conforming us to himself by his Spirit.

Our Christian lives are like a pilgrimage. The road is not easy. But we are moving toward a city in which we dwell with God for ever. The apostle John's vision of the future should be firmly fixed in our gaze as we walk through this life:

> He will wipe away every tear from their eyes, and death will be no more, neither shall there be mourning, nor crying, nor pain anymore, for the former things have passed away. And he who was seated on the throne said, 'Behold, I am making all things new' (Rev. 21:4, 5b).

# Further Reading

### *Where to Start*

Jerry Bridges, *The Pursuit of Holiness* (Carol Stream, IL: NavPress, 2016).

David Powlison, *How Does Sanctification Work?* (Wheaton: Crossway, 2017).

John Bunyan, *The Fear of God* (repr. Edinburgh: Banner of Truth Trust, 2018).

Michael Horton, *Putting Amazing Back Into Grace* (Grand Rapids: Zondervan, 2011 revised edition).

J. C. Ryle, *Holiness: Its Nature, Hindrances, Difficulties and Roots* (repr. Edinburgh: Banner of Truth Trust, 2014).

### *In More Detail*

James Montgomery Boice and Philip Graham Ryken, *The Doctrines of Grace* (Wheaton, Crossway, 2009).

Sinclair B. Ferguson, *Devoted to God: Blueprints for Sanctification* (Edinburgh: Banner of Truth, 2016).

John Owen, *The Mortification of Sin*, ed. & abr. by Richard Rushing (Edinburgh: Banner of Truth Trust, 2004).

John Owen, *Indwelling Sin in Believers* (Edinburgh: Banner of Truth Trust, 2010).

## *The Bigger Picture*

Michael Allen, *Sanctification* (Grand Rapids: Zondervan, 2017).

William Gurnall, *The Christian in Complete Armour* (repr. London: Banner of Truth Trust, 1964).

# Banner Mini-Guides